LET'S GO IN

LET'S GO IN

My Journey to a University Presidency

T. Alan Hurwitz

Gallaudet University Press
Washington, DC

Washington, DC 20002
http://gupress.gallaudet.edu

Paperback ISBN 978-1-944838-62-1
Ebook ISBN 978-1-944838-63-8
Manifold ISBN 978-1-944838-80-5

Cover design by Eric C. Wilder. Front cover image by Cedric B. Egeli. *President T. Alan Hurwitz*, 2015. Oil on canvas, original dimensions 50 x 34 inches. Gift to Gallaudet University by the Gallaudet University Alumni Association through the Laurent Clerc Cultural Fund. Reproduced with permission.

Library of Congress Cataloging-in-Publication Data

Names: Hurwitz, T. Alan, 1942– author.
Title: Let's go in : my journey to a university presidency / T. Alan
   Hurwitz.
Description: Washington, DC : Gallaudet University Press, [2020] | Summary:
   Deaf president of Gallaudet University, 2010-2015. Also served as
   president of National Technical Institute for the Deaf.
Identifiers: LCCN 2019012592 | ISBN 9781944838621 (pbk. : alk. paper) |
   ISBN 9781944838638 (e-book)
Subjects: LCSH: Hurwitz, T. Alan, 1942– | Deaf—United States—Biography
   | Gallaudet University—Presidents. | National Technical Institute for the
   Deaf—Presidents. | Deaf—Education—United States. | College
   presidents—United States—Biography. | College presidents—Washington
   (D.C.)—Biography. | Jewish college presidents—United
   States—Biography. | Jewish college presidents—Washington
   (D.C.)—Biography.
Classification: LCC HV2534.H87 A3 2020 | DDC 378.753092 [B]—dc23
LC record available at https://lccn.loc.gov/2019012592

To my parents
Juliette Ruth Kahn Hurwitz and Harold Allen Hurwitz

Contents

Foreword

I HAVE KNOWN Alan for twenty-seven years. But have I really known him?

It is true that I have observed him conduct meetings; make presentations; circulate among friends and colleagues at receptions and dinners; interact with deaf and hearing faculty, students, and university administrators; and work with community leaders. We have had one-on-one meetings. We have bowled together. His name, persona, and engagements have come up in my conversations with others.

I thought I knew Alan. Then I read his memoir. And reread it. Yes, a lot of what I knew about him emerged in this memoir. But, as I enthusiastically learned, there is so much more.

Alan is not afraid, as so many of us are, to reveal himself from the inside out—from his heart, soul, and inner self.

The reader learns of Alan's earliest years, his challenges, successes, and disappointments at every stage of his life's path. He is candid and, at times, most introspective about his fears, ambitions, and innermost feelings.

He paints a comprehensive fabric of his ancestral heritage—starting with his loving and ever-present parents, and progressing to his grandparents, great grandparents, uncles, and aunts—who they all are, where they are from, and what they did in their lives. Throughout the memoir, they appear and reappear as mentors and partners, advising and supporting him, and serving as role models. Alan reflects their values and religion, and these attributes have shaped who he is and underlie his remarkable lifetime accomplishments.

He offers this background in his humble and modest style, which causes the reader to sometimes merge their persona with Alan's, thereby experiencing his dilemmas and circumstances as if they were their own. There are times when the reader so identifies with Alan that they anxiously await the next paragraph or page to reveal itself.

Above all, Alan speaks over and over again about his devotion to and admiration for his wife, Vicki. They have both been deaf since birth. They started dating when she was a sophomore in high school and he a freshman in college. You can say that they grew up together, informing and learning from each other. They married the year (1965) he graduated (at age twenty-two) with his bachelor's degree from Washington University in St. Louis.

Vicki is the love of his life, his best friend, closest confidant and partner, and true soul mate. While tremendously successful and accomplished professionally, Alan and Vicki hold their family fabric as clearly their most cherished reason for living. Their children (Bernard and Stephanie/Stefi), grandchildren, siblings, parents, grandparents, and other family members are always in their hearts and minds.

Over the years, Alan and Vicki have developed very close friendships—both personal and professional—with many individuals coast to coast and around the world. They are part of their extended family. Each of these individuals is mentioned by name (surname, given name, or nickname) several times throughout the memoir, many of them appearing both early and late in the flow of Alan's life story.

Alan's work ethic has few equals, and that extends from his young days delivering newspapers house to house on his bicycle, to later as a computer programmer working in the FORTRAN language, and, finally, to his days as a faculty member, administrator, and community advocate. He is quick and ready to give full credit to others, of all stripes and roles, for their contributions, large and small. One has the impression that he is underplaying his own unique creativity, risk-taking, and overall contributions.

At each step of the ladder of professional advancement, Alan has not shied away from making hard decisions to foster needed change on the academic, fiscal, and administrative sides of Gallaudet University and the National Technical Institute for the Deaf at Rochester Institute of Technology (RIT/NTID). He has done this consistently through a process of shared governance, in which he speaks to and (especially) listens to students, faculty, administrators, alumni, and members of the community at large. He both informs and learns, gaining and sharing knowledge in the process, arriving at decisions, and taking actions that are much improved over what they would have been without the listening and informing. This process does not necessarily lead to a majority vote decision. Instead, the person who will be held accountable for the decision takes responsibility for making the decision. While not everyone may agree with the decision, they support the action because of the process utilized.

This shared governance approach is an integral part of Alan's work ethic, his ethical underpinnings, his sense of humor, his upbringing by his devoted parents, his later education leading to a bachelor's degree, and, ultimately, a doctorate, and his professional experience and expertise. This model has allowed him to lead two great institutions for deaf and hard of hearing students—for six years as president of Gallaudet University and forty years at RIT/NTID. He guided these institutions to major new, societally relevant, and important summits, and even higher expectations for the future. Following the lead of his trustees at Gallaudet, Alan truly looks for "big ideas" and moves aggressively to realize them. For example, at Gallaudet, he established a doctoral program in interpretation and translation, a doctoral program in educational neuroscience, and preprofessional programs in four career areas.

Alan is a wonderful role model for deaf, hard of hearing, and hearing students and professionals across the full human diversity spectrum. He is committed, in particular, to the growth and success of deaf and hard of hearing individuals, and this commitment is illustrated by his leadership roles in numerous local, national, and international organizations and associations serving deaf and hard of hearing individuals.

Alan concludes his memoir by reflecting in general on his forty-six-year journey in higher education, centering his thoughts and recommendations on leadership skills. All of this discussion is very much worth reviewing and absorbing.

Two aspects of Alan's memoir resonate especially with me. First is his discussion of the critical function of highly trained interpreters.

This issue is especially important to Alan, given the fact that he grew up in and had to cope with a world without interpreters. And in college, he was forced to rely on volunteer classmates to take notes for him. Things have improved much since then, but even more can be done on a broader scale.

The second reflection I would like to comment on is Alan's observation of why Gallaudet and NTID have six or seven times (on an institutional percentage basis) as many students transferring to them as other colleges and universities have. He points out that the college experience must be more than books, labs, lectures, and examinations. Students must also have the opportunity outside of the classroom to interact with one another in a mutually reinforcing social and interpersonal context. They need to have time to develop their leadership skills and form a personal network that can extend over a lifetime. Student government, intercollegiate athletics, student publications, and clubs are a critical part of the overall collegiate learning experience. For deaf and hard of hearing students, the dimensions of their learning development may be arduous at the typical university, where the vast majority of students are hearing and unaware of Deaf culture. Institutions like Gallaudet and NTID provide opportunities for their students to realize this complete educational focus. Upon graduation, students will more readily possess the leadership, socialization, teamwork, and communication attributes that will facilitate their success in both the deaf and hearing worlds.

To sum it all up, this memoir offers an intriguingly touching story of one person's journey through life, as well as an extremely valuable prescription for personal and professional success. Everyone, both deaf and hearing, will love the story. Everyone, both deaf and hearing, will profit from the observations and recommendations emanating from the story. It takes courage and self-confidence to bare one's soul and provide a light into one's deepest thoughts. Dr. T. Alan Hurwitz demonstrates, in his memoir, that he has both.

Albert J. Simone
President Emeritus
Rochester Institute of Technology

Preface

THIS BOOK OF MEMORIES and commentaries is dedicated to my parents, Juliette Ruth (née Kahn) and Harold Allen Hurwitz. They worked hard all their lives and made a lot of sacrifices to ensure that I was given opportunities to experience all the twists and turns that I might confront during my lifetime.

My mother showed me many articles about successful deaf adults and told me that if they could do it, then I could do it, too. She also introduced me to deaf adults who were leaders in the Deaf community. She and I always had interesting and intellectual discussions about anything and everything; she was truly ahead of the times as a woman. While most women of her generation stayed home as a homemaker, my mother always worked and, at the same time, managed to take care of the family and tend to our home. She also was the family bookkeeper and made decisions as the "head of the family."

My father taught me a lot about sports, which led me to develop a passion for playing and watching sports. We also played many board and number games, and these instilled in me a love of math. My father taught me a great deal about the importance of a strong work ethic. He was always on time at work and never missed a day, even when he did not feel well. He was a very patient man who loved to tease people. He was not afraid to talk with hearing people; he would carry on conversations with them by writing notes on his notepad.

My retirement from Gallaudet University at the end of December 2015 marked the culmination of fifty-plus years in my professional life. Once we settled back in our home, my dear wife, Vicki, my family, and several close friends encouraged me to write a memoir of my personal and professional life. I was initially reluctant to write or even talk about myself. But then I became convinced that my story could inspire deaf and hard of hearing people and people with disabilities to aim for their highest goals. Bless Vicki—she kept encouraging me to start by making a long list of things I should include in the memoir. Within two months, I finally started to jot down some ideas, and the outline came out to thirty-five pages. It took me nearly nine months before I could sit down and begin to write the memoir because I struggled with how to translate the outline into a narrative. I ultimately decided to put it aside, and, with time, I started to record what I could recall from my early years, without thought to any structure.

As I pondered my journey through life, I want to give credit to my parents, especially my mother, who did not have much education but who, enthusiastically and passionately, encouraged me to aim for the best education possible to prepare myself for a successful personal and professional life. I begin my story with my family and early education, followed by my professional careers in engineering and higher education. I reveal the roads I have taken, the triumphs and defeats, and the lessons I learned that led me to the places where I have been. My ultimate goal is to offer insights for families and professionals that can inspire young deaf and hard of hearing people to achieve their dreams and goals and manage the trials and tribulations they will face in their lives.

When I was growing up and developing my professional skills, I had no idea I would arrive at the places where I have been. My ambition has always been to excel in whatever I aspired to do. I loved my work as an engineer and computer programmer. I enjoyed working with young people and inspiring them to do their best and reach their potential. Teaching and advising students was a passion, and I expected to continue in these roles for the duration of my professional life. I also cherished the times I spent in the Deaf community, especially in the various leadership roles I held in different organizations. I never dreamed, nor had the ambition, for progressive leadership roles in higher education or for becoming a university president.

The reader may note that many of the incidents I describe may appear disjointed and unrelated. I have done my best to flesh out scenes and characters so that readers may understand that these incidents were integral parts of my journey. I hope that the memoir reveals the events and experiences that affected my life and led me to what I accomplished. It includes both good and bad experiences, the challenges I faced, and the lessons learned from them. I desire to let the readers know what I was thinking, as well as why and how I made certain decisions in my administrative roles. I have attempted to talk briefly about certain people—family, friends, and colleagues—who played important roles in my life.

I believe Abraham Lincoln's quote, "In the end, it's not the years in your life that count. It's the life in your years," sums up my experiences in building a foundation that allowed me to progress in leadership roles over my lifetime. It is my hope that my journey will inspire and show young deaf people how achievements can lead to unexpected accomplishments.

A Note about the Title

As you'll read in this book, my journey to the Gallaudet presidency was a long and sometimes rocky one. Throughout everything, my beloved wife Vicki was at my side, supporting me and helping to make it happen while she pursued her own career. On the day we arrived at Gallaudet, I paused at the front gate and asked her if she really wanted to take this on or if we should turn around and drive back to Rochester, back to all our friends and our familiar routines. With her characteristic enthusiasm, she smiled at me, squeezed my hand, and said, "Let's go in!"

Acknowledgments

MOST OF ALL, I am forever indebted to Vicki T. Hurwitz, my best friend and loving wife for more than fifty-five years, the devoted mother of Bernard and Stephanie, and the devoted grandmother to our grandchildren Susan Juliette and Ethan. Vicki was instrumental in helping me wade through the large collection of pictures, articles, publications, and memories that were shared with us by our families, friends, and professional colleagues. Being a pack rat, I saved most of the papers and documents from my nearly forty years at the National Technical Institute for the Deaf at Rochester Institute of Technology and my six years as president of Gallaudet University. I also saved a great deal of material from my involvement in community organizations.

I am grateful to individuals at Gallaudet University who helped me write this memoir. Ivey Wallace, my editor at Gallaudet University Press, was patient with my being a novice book author, and she gave me a lot of helpful tips to improve my writing. Michael Olson, the now-retired head archivist at Gallaudet, and his staff were invaluable in organizing the papers I donated to the Gallaudet University Archives. I am indebted to Vicki, Stacy Lawrence, Mark Benjamin, NTID's photographer, Emily Hopkins, and Lezlie "Zhee" Chatmon, a Gallaudet University photographer, who were very helpful in locating photographs for the memoir. Deirdre Mullervy, the managing editor, and Katie Lee, the acquisitions editor, at Gallaudet University Press, were very helpful with preparing the photographs for the manuscript. Angela Leppig, the director of the press, was helpful with the marketing aspects of the book. Credit also goes to the RIT Digital Archives for digitizing photos of my years at RIT/NTID.

I also want to thank Don Beil, Paul Ogden, Harry Lang, and my family for making themselves available to discuss and critique my ideas for the memoir.

I often have been asked to name the role models and mentors who influenced me during my early years as well as in my adult life. I can honestly say there are too many to mention here, but they all have my thanks and gratitude. I cherish the opportunities I had to work with many different people and to hire direct reports who were smarter and more experienced than me. I sincerely believe that over the years, because of these folks, I developed strong listening skills that allowed me to work collaboratively with diverse individuals. Many of these role models and mentors are mentioned throughout the memoir.

1

"You Can Be Anything You Want to Be"

DURING THE INTERMISSION, I excused myself to go to the men's room. When the swinging door closed behind me, my Blackberry started to buzz—and kept buzzing. Incoming was a long list of texts from Ben Soukup and Frank Wu, chair and vice chair, respectively, of the Gallaudet board, who had been trying to reach me for over an hour. They wanted to meet with me right away. Where was I? they wanted to know. Flustered, I stood at the sink and responded, texting them that I'd been in a hotel ballroom with no cell reception all evening. "We'd like to talk to you right away," they replied. I texted back: "OK, I'll find a way back to my hotel now, but there are hundreds of people at this event, so it won't be that easy to leave inconspicuously."

"That's understandable," they texted, "but come as soon as you can."

Back in the ballroom, I tried to get my wife Vicki's attention. Characteristically, she was surrounded by a crowd, talking with her friends. Her sociability and interest in people, usually something I especially love and admire in her, frustrated me at that moment. Couldn't she be more retiring? More standoffish, so that it would be easier to extricate her quickly from crowds when time was of the essence? She finally saw me, and I silently—and I hoped unobtrusively—mouthed to her that we needed to leave right away. "What for? Why?" she asked. I mouthed again, "We have to leave. Don't argue with me."

I remembered that our daughter was in the hallway outside the ballroom, so I added, "Stefi wants to see you in the hall. And bring our coats!" Of course, when we got into the crowded hall, Vicki and Stefi saw each other and immediately began what looked like a leisurely conversation. I gently tugged Vicki away but still couldn't explain why we had to leave so abruptly. A ride down the slow escalator to the lobby deposited us into another large crowd of deaf people because the event was a Deaf community function, sponsored by Purple, a video-relay services vendor. "Hello!" "Hi, how are you?" "Good to see you, Dr. Hurwitz!" "Have you gotten any news about the search decision yet?" We smiled as we made a beeline to the exit. I felt perspiration gathering on my forehead.

Earlier in the day, I'd had my first meeting with the Gallaudet University Board of Trustees (after two earlier meetings with the search committee and one campus-wide public meeting), and this was my third visit to Gallaudet as a presidential candidate. When the meeting had ended at two-thirty, Ben and Frank had asked me to meet with them privately in the next room.

"We'll be making our selection this afternoon," Ben said, "and so our last question of you and all the other candidates is this: If you are selected, will you accept our offer?" I'd known I was past the point of no return. I *did* want the job and would accept it if it were offered to me. It would be the leadership opportunity of a lifetime, a thrilling cap to an already unexpected career. "Yes," I said.

Later, at lunch with my wife, I shared everything with her, including my assessment of my chances. I'd done well, I thought, at my last interview. The board members and I had been candid and comfortable in our discussion of how critical a time it was in the university's trajectory, with a newly written strategic plan and the selection of a president to manifest the plan through organizational leadership. "It will be a tough decision for the board," I told her, "because the other finalists are such outstanding candidates."

The others were Dr. Stephen Weiner, provost of Gallaudet University; Dr. Roslyn Rosen, director of the National Center on Deafness at California State University, Northridge; and Dr. Ronald Stern, superintendent of the New Mexico School for the Deaf. Since all were either alumni of Gallaudet or current leaders, I had initially wondered why I was included in the final pool, especially since I had not attended Gallaudet. It also occurred to me that *not* being selected as Gallaudet's president might be a blessing in disguise because it would mean I could remain at the National Institute for the Deaf at the Rochester Institute of Technology (RIT/NTID), where I'd happily spent nearly forty years of my career. But after the months of interviews—meeting with large groups of lively, engaged Gallaudet students, meeting faculty and the board of trustees, seeing the campus, imagining ourselves living in this city, and leading this vibrant university into its next promising chapter—the prospect of having RIT/NTID as the last stop on my professional journey paled.

Outside, it was still pouring rain, and there was a long line of folks waiting under the hotel portico for a cab. Red and green and blue lights reflected on the wet sidewalks and streets. As soon as I saw an opening in the taxi line, we cut in, excusing ourselves, and finally got into a car. We were on our way at last! I wrote a note to the driver to take us to our Marriott hotel a mile away, and then I showed Vicki the long list of texts on my Blackberry. Her face showed alarm and apprehension that matched my own.

I texted Ben and Frank that we were finally in a cab, and they responded that they were in the bar on the second floor of the Courtyard Washington, DC/US Capitol hotel in the NoMa district. "Should I come alone?" I texted. If they said yes, that might be an indication they'd decided not to select me and didn't want to break the bad news with my wife there. They texted back: "No, bring Vicki, and we'll all have drinks together." That seemed like a good sign.

Ben and Frank were nursing cocktails when we arrived, sitting around a large table by the bar, next to a window that looked out onto city lights blurred in the rain. Smiling, they urged us to order drinks too. When the waitress returned from the bar with our glasses, Ben grinned widely and said at last, "Alan, I'm delighted to let you know that the board has decided to appoint you as the tenth president of Gallaudet University!"

Vicki and I turned to look at each other, completely stunned. I looked questioningly around, and Vicki said, "Yes!" Ben smiled and asked if we were surprised. When we said yes, he said, "Let's celebrate," and toasted us.

The vice chair, Frank Yu, then produced a contract for me to review and sign. When I'd read it, signed my name, and pushed the contract back across the table to him, Frank said, "Did you have a nice lunch at Five Guys?" Vicki and I again looked at each other, puzzled, and asked how he'd known that we'd grabbed lunch at that burger place earlier in the day. He grinned and said it was posted on Twitter by a student member of the presidential search committee. Our lives had shifted into a new phase, a very public one. Our privacy was shot for the foreseeable future.

Still dazed, though thrilled and happy, Vicki and I went up to our room and texted our children the good news, asking them to keep it to themselves until after the announcement. I immediately went to work on my acceptance speech at the round table in the corner of our hotel room, staring at the blank screen of my laptop for a moment, conscious of a feeling of great joy and gratitude. My mind kept returning, for some reason, to my father, who always proudly referred to me as "my boy." What would he have thought, to see his boy about to take the reins of the world's premier institution of learning and research for deaf and hard of hearing scholars and students, the first born-deaf person to lead the school? I could picture his face, his loving look, and reassuring smile, his confidence in me. My parents' spirit of pride and optimism had a lot to do with where I found myself now.

2

Our Roots

LIKE ME, both my parents were born deaf (or had been deaf as long as they could remember), but unlike me, they were born into hearing families. My paternal grandparents, Ben and Rose, hadn't known anything about raising deaf children, nor where and how deaf children could be educated, so they kept my father and his hard of hearing sister, my Aunt Cranie, at home above their grocery store in Sioux City, Iowa. They were Yiddish and Russian speakers with very little English, who found it doubly difficult to communicate with or about their deaf children who were growing up in an English-speaking country.

My mother's grandparents and my father's parents all came to the United States from Central and Eastern Europe in the 1800s. Like most European Jews of the time, they made the trip to escape poverty and persecution. My paternal grandfather, Baruch Gurevich, was born on September 29, 1885, in Chavusi, Belarus. He escaped from Czarist Russia in the late 1890s and landed at Ellis Island in New York. He couldn't read or write English. When the clerk asked his name, he might have thought my grandfather said "Hurwitz," and that became his legal name. His first name, Baruch, was changed to Benjamin, and everyone called him Ben.

Although he worked as a tie peddler at first, Ben had an adventurous spirit and soon joined the wave of western migration, probably with intentions to dig for gold. On his way to California, he stopped in Sioux City, Iowa, where he met a young woman named Rose Mazie, my grandmother. She had also been born in Belarus, on February 20, 1892, in Klyetsk, Minsk, and had arrived in America with her parents in the mid-1880s, where they settled in Iowa for reasons lost to us now. Her parents most likely had connections among the large Jewish immigrant community in Sioux City. (Their neighborhood was home to famed twin advice columnists Pauline and Esther Friedman, whose syndicated columns were known as Dear Abby and Ask Ann Landers, and whose parents were Russian Jewish immigrants as well.)

Since my father's sister, Aunt Cranie, had some usable hearing, she could lipread her parents better than my father could. My father, however, never learned Yiddish, and his communication with his own parents and neighbors was limited to gestures.

I don't know what would have become of my father if his life had stayed on this limited path. Luckily, in 1926, when he was thirteen

Ben and Rose Hurwitz, my paternal grandparents.

years old, my grandparents learned about the Iowa School for the Deaf (ISD), and they enrolled him there. The school was eighty miles south in Council Bluffs, so my grandparents drove him to the school every fall and picked him up for the holidays in December and the summer months. Finally, he was receiving a formal education. It did not take my father long to learn sign language, make many friends, and become an outstanding student and a standout basketball player who also loved playing tennis and baseball. He loved ISD and thrived there, but his sister, who attended ISD for one year, was unhappy at school and returned home to public school in Sioux City, where she dropped out before graduating high school, a very common outcome for a deaf student in the 1930s.

ISD, like many other residential schools at that time, had a rigorous academic program. My father took high school courses in English, mathematics, chemistry, and physics. He also took several vocational courses that prepared him for jobs as a baker, Linotype operator, and furniture maker. Graduating at the age of twenty-five, he took the entrance exams to attend Gallaudet College and passed. But soon, new circumstances, and his priorities, would keep him from ever attending.

MY MOTHER, JULIETTE, was born on January 15, 1916, the daughter of two first-generation Kansans. Her mother, Rosaline Berlau, was a native of Leavenworth, Kansas and the daughter of two Polish immigrants. Her father, a dashing man named Tobias Kahn, was the son of immigrants from Bohemia. My mother was always an active child, playing ball, loving to climb trees, and preferring the outdoors to staying inside. In contrast, her hearing sister, Sylvia, was a bookworm. But the two sisters were always close.

How my mother became deaf and whether she was born hearing remains unknown. My grandparents did not realize she was deaf until she was five years old, when a deaf nine-year-old neighbor, Elizabeth Shannon, told them she thought Juliette was deaf. Soon after, my grandparents enrolled her at the Madison School in Kansas City, which had an oral program for deaf children. My mother and her sister communicated well because Sylvia was an excellent lipreader.

Roslyn (Ga-Ga) Kahn, my maternal grandmother.

And then, when my mother was ten, her parents sent her to the Central Institute for the Deaf (CID) in St. Louis. The school had opened its doors just a little over a decade earlier, in 1914, and was founded by Max Aaron Goldstein, an Austrian-educated American physician. He aimed to teach deaf children to speak orally. By the time my mother was sent there, the school had erected new buildings and had a wait list for enrollment. Unfortunately, after about a year at CID, she became very ill with thyroid problems and left to have surgery and recuperate. She spent the remainder of her middle school education at the Madison School back at home. But when she was seventeen, she asked her mother, my grandmother Rosaline (we called her Ga-Ga), if she could return to CID, where my mother felt that she could get a better education. In all her years at school, my mother still had not learned to read! When she saw Sylvia with her nose in a book, she sometimes wondered what that would feel like to be able to sit for hours, immersed in a story. What was the trick to reading, she wondered?

Her primary teacher upon her return to CID was Mrs. Jessie Skinner, the mother of deaf twin sons who were also CID students. Mrs. Skinner struggled to teach my mother how to read, but with little suc-

Tobias Kahn, my maternal grandfather.

cess. Finally, Mrs. Skinner told my mother that if she didn't become literate, she would be sent home. Terrified, my mother picked up the novel *Little Women,* determined to read it word by word. It was slow going at first, but after a while, she began to visualize the story of the four March sisters—their cozy house, their loves and literary ambitions, Beth's battle with illness, and the dramatic plays Jo wrote and directed in the attic. When my mother began to picture the characters and settings in her mind, she was finally inspired to keep reading, to stay in that world, and discover what happened next. She told me that as soon as she finished *Little Women,* she picked up a second book, and then another. Soon, like Aunt Sylvia, she was a true fan of reading, and it was a love that would last her whole life, and one that she would work steadily to instill in me.

When she graduated from CID, my mother entered ninth grade in a public school in Kansas City. By then, she was nineteen and thought herself too old to be in high school, so she left after just a few months and went to work.

It was a few years later that she met my father, who was visiting his aunt, Elizabeth Mazie Shapiro, in Kansas City. Aunt Elizabeth knew my mother's great-aunt Emma Berlau, so they played a role in introducing them to each other.

My father had just graduated from ISD and planned to attend Gallaudet College in Washington, DC, at the end of the summer. Although my mother didn't know sign language and my father didn't speak or lipread, they somehow managed to fall quickly and deeply in love. How they communicated with each other is a mystery. My father decided to forgo his college education in favor of settling down with my mother, and they married on October 6, 1938, when my mother was twenty-two years old, and my father was twenty-five. Over time, my mother became proficient in sign language, and my father learned how to lipread my mother. It takes two to tango, I guess!

Soon after the wedding, they moved from Kansas City to Topeka, where my father got a job as a Linotype operator at a newspaper. After one year, they moved to Orange City, Iowa, where he again worked as a Linotype operator. They stayed in Orange City for three years before moving to Sioux City, where my father got a job as a baker, another skill he had learned at ISD. They lived with my father's parents for a while before moving to an apartment on Pierce Street. My mother was a homemaker, and she soon learned her way around Sioux City and made new friends in the Deaf community.

On September 17, 1942, I was born, their first and only child. Following the Jewish custom of naming children after a deceased family member, typically using the first initial of the person's name, my parents decided to name me after my mother's father, Tobias Kahn. He got the H1N1 virus in the 1918 pandemic and died of rheumatic fever and a heart attack (a common complication of the virus) just before my mother's sixteenth birthday when he was only forty-seven years old. Later, my father told me that they'd wanted to name me Thomas or Theodore, but they couldn't pronounce either name well enough to be understood by the attending nurse. She wrote down "Tracy?" and my mother liked it. My parents then added Alan as my middle name, since my paternal grandfather's middle name was Allan, and my father's middle name was Allen.

SIOUX CITY, a medium-sized city in the flat grasslands of northwestern Iowa, is bordered on its south by a meandering Missouri River. The Sioux City metropolitan area includes cities in three states: Sioux City, Iowa; South Sioux City, Nebraska; and North Sioux City, South Dakota. It was a homey and convenient place to grow up, with at least one of everything we needed—stores, banks, gas stations, car dealerships, museums, hospitals, a big library, bowling alleys, and many parks. A popular refrain in our town was, "If it's more than a ten-minute drive, it's too far."

I was lucky to have been born into a supportive and loving family. My parents nurtured and protected me, and I never wanted to disappoint them.

One of my earliest memories in Sioux City is of a chilly afternoon when I was three years old. My parents took me with my tricycle to Grandview Park, where there was an outdoor opera band shell with a small pond in front of it. I was having fun pedaling around on the sidewalks uphill from the band shell when suddenly I lost control and started coasting downhill toward the stage and the pond. I picked up speed. The cold air bit my ears and pushed against my face. My little trike was hopping and bouncing with each bump and dip on the frozen grass. I had never ridden so fast in my life, and I had no clue how to stop. I hurtled down the steep hill toward the stage and pond until my trike hit the retaining wall and threw me into the air. I flipped and landed flat on my back in the frigid water. Looking up, I saw the big, gray sky and geese flying. Then my parents' faces were there above me, looking down at me with horror and relief. They swooped me up out of the water, stripped my wet coat off of me, and wrapped me up in their own dry coats. We hurried back home to warm up, and they fussed over me and fed me hot tea. I had never seen my parents so worried as they'd looked at that moment in the pond, nor realized before that I was vulnerable in any way.

Growing up, I knew the city's layout well—a downtown business district surrounded by residential neighborhoods, which were ringed by stockyards where farmers would haul their livestock for processing. Beyond the stockyards was farmland. It took me five minutes to ride my bicycle from our home to my grandparents' house. Whenever we drove in our car near the stockyards, I would make faces, cover my

Mom and Dad with me when I was two years old.

nose, and hold my breath because the smell was so horrible. My parents laughed at my reaction and explained to me what was happening at the processing center. "This is where the trucks deliver cattle to the stockyards, and each animal is slaughtered here. Afterward," they told me, "the carcass is hung on big hooks hanging from the ceiling, and aged to allow the enzymes to increase meat tenderness before the carcasses are butchered into the cuts sold at stores."

"Oh," I thought. "Good to know." I liked learning how the world worked. My parents knew so much.

When I was seven, I got a new bike that I rode all over the neighborhood. One day, a neighbor boy, Mike, who was nine or ten, told me to follow him on his bike. Sure! I thought. We rode down the hill from my grandparents' home through downtown, past warehouses where there were eighteen-wheeler trucks parked in neat rows. We continued riding—under the parked vehicles and onto a long bridge crossing the Missouri River. I kept following Mike. I felt that we'd been riding for hours, but I wasn't tired, and I was seeing fresh new sights—bridges, fields. Then, up ahead, I noticed a huge sign welcoming us to South Sioux City, Nebraska. Whoa! We had biked five miles from my grandparents' home.

Upon seeing the sign, I immediately knew it was wrong to go that far without my parents' knowledge, let alone cross the state line. "I'm going back!" I told Mike, but he said he would keep on going. I wheeled around and headed for home, pedaling as fast as I could back past the warehouses, under the trucks, through downtown, and up the hill. My parents were there waiting for me, furious that I had been gone so long. "I was following Mike, and I didn't know where we were going until I saw the sign!" I told them. "You're grounded," they told me, sending me straight to my bedroom without dinner. I sat on my bed feeling terrible, remembering the looks on their faces and imagining how they must have felt not knowing where I'd disappeared to. A half-hour later, my mother came into my room and beckoned me down for dinner, after all. "I guess you need to eat," she said, "after such a long journey."

IN 1946, when I was four, I was sent to live 500 miles away at CID, my mother's alma mater in St. Louis. Even though my father had benefited greatly from his years at the closer ISD, he was concerned that ISD no longer offered the college preparatory courses that he had taken. So he concurred with my mother that it was worth being farther away to get a better education. My mother was a prime example: She had strong speaking skills and could easily communicate with my dad's hearing parents and his extended family while he couldn't. "Why not send him to ISD? It's only an hour-and-a-half drive away!" my parents' friends argued. But my parents stood firm.

As soon as they enrolled me in the school, the principal, Dr. Helen S. Lane, asked my parents to stop using sign language with me, even though I had never signed much with them anyway. My parents agreed, and from then on, my mother and I would always talk with each other orally. She was an excellent lipreader, and we had an effortless time communicating with each other.

"I am going to take you to a very good school, the same school I went to when I was little," my mother told me. "It is a few hours from here, in St. Louis," she explained. It was going to be an exciting journey, she promised. We would be riding on a train. We'd first drive to Council Bluffs and then get on a train to St. Louis, going through Kansas City and Jefferson City, Missouri.

She let me have the window seat, and I watched the fields and shining lakes rush by, black and white cows in vast pastures, little towns and the back edges of cities, where the houses were crowded together under drooping power lines and cars were parked close together along the streets. We had a picnic of roast beef sandwiches and potato chips in the dining car, and I took naps.

When we arrived at CID, the school looked interesting—bright and clean. Everyone we met was friendly. My mother and I were introduced to other mothers and fathers and children, to teachers and dorm parents. Mother hugged and kissed Mrs. Skinner, her old reading teacher, who still taught at CID. "This is the field I played in when I was a girl," my mother told me, pointing out a window. But eventually, she knelt to say goodbye to me, reminding me I'd be coming home over the holidays. I began to cry and couldn't stop crying. Out of the corner of my eye, I could see my green plaid suitcase, which was packed with my long pants, shirts, sweaters, and pajamas, and a few of my favorite picture books.

Although she had tried to explain (at home and then again on our train ride) that I would be staying at the school without her, I didn't want her to leave. She hugged me so tightly that it hurt a little, and I breathed in her familiar smell. When she let me go to look into my crying face, I saw that her face was sad too. She hugged me to her again, told me she loved me, stood up, and walked away.

I stopped crying when I realized there were ten other boys in my dorm room to play with.

3

At Home at the Central Institute for the Deaf

February 6, 1956

My Beloved Parents:

Did "Skippy" stay at my grandparents' home when everybody was gone?

Saturday afternoon, Johnny Thomson, Bill Jordan, Derek Sweeting, a boy from Canada, and I stayed here. The rest went to the movie. We didn't go to the movie because we didn't want to. From 1 till 3 o'clock, we went with the older boys to the park to go sleigh riding. When we came back, we went to the Barber Shop. I had not had a haircut since the first week of December. My hair was quite long. Before our hair was cut, we had some hamburger sandwiches and hot cocoa. Now I look a little bit different because of my hair.

How's everybody in Sioux City? I wrote a card to Gary Baumann.

Thank you very much for the package of Valentine cards.

My black shoes aren't too small. They fit just right. I use the play shoes for the rubbers. The rubbers fit my play shoes perfectly.

Sunday night, we had movies in the auditorium. One of the films was just what I wanted to see. It was about the "Kennel-Ling." It was about all kinds of dogs.

Now Steve Mirsky uses only one crutch.

Saturday night we had a dancing lesson. We learned how to Jitterbug.

Your loving son,
Tracy Alan

EVERY YEAR FOR TEN YEARS, between the ages of four and thirteen, I looked forward to traveling back and forth from home to St. Louis by way of Council Bluffs in September, December, and June. It was a long ride, more than ten hours, but I loved sleeping in the Pullman car overnight. Sometimes, late at night, I would get out of my bunk to go to the bathroom but then take the opportunity to prolong my exploration of the train as it swayed down the track, the night sky outside above rushing fields. And in the daytime, you could walk a bit past other passengers and see all the families and businesspeople traveling with you.

During one of my trips when I was about eight or nine years old, a group of distinguished men came on board our train in Jefferson City, and a tall gentleman with white hair and a gray suit sat down opposite me. He had a very kind face and soft eyes that crinkled at the corners, and he tried gamely to talk with me. I couldn't read his lips, so I just nodded my head and smiled as if I understood him. Did he understand that I was deaf? I couldn't tell. He continued to talk to me all the way until the next stop in Independence, Missouri. When the train halted, he stood up and very formally offered to shake my hand. "It was nice to meet you," he said as we shook hands—that much I could decipher—and then he got off the train. I looked outside and, as the train began to pull away from the platform, I was dumbfounded to see a station billboard declaring "Home of Harry S. Truman" illustrated with a large oval portrait of the very man with whom I'd been riding. The gentle-looking white-haired man who had spent so long trying to converse with me had been President Truman! (This, of course, is a true story, but I regret that I didn't ask for his autograph so that more people would believe me.)

Living in a dorm with ten "brothers" was never boring or lonely, although it was likely a challenge for our housemother, who had her room adjoining our sleeping quarters. Many times, she had to come into our room after bedtime to urge us to stop playing and get some sleep.

We came from all over the country: Georgia, Texas, Florida, Ohio, Kentucky, Illinois, California, and so forth. Even though we ranged in ages and grades, we were close friends. Every week, we'd have a field trip to a library or the YMCA. St. Louis was a beautiful city—five times bigger than Sioux City. Like my hometown, it was a flat river city, with the Missouri and Mississippi Rivers meeting not far outside its city limits. On weekends, we'd play in nearby Forest Park, go to St. Louis Cardinals baseball games at the old Sportsman's Park, visit museums, and play games in the dorm or on the fenced and sheltered roof.

At mealtimes, we sat at a long rectangular table with five seats on each side and a supervisor and a teaching assistant on each end. I thought the food was terrible, but breakfast is hard to mess up, and so it became my favorite meal of the day. "I'll take that soft-boiled egg, if you're not going to eat it," I'd say, and several of my egg-averse roommates would hand them over to me. In this way, I managed to consume the majority of my daily calories before noon.

One dinner, when I was about eleven or twelve years old, I was sitting next to a teacher-in-training who was new and didn't know me well. I was feeling sick to my stomach and didn't think I could eat the peas on my plate, although I usually liked peas. I asked, "Could I please be excused?"

"No," said the teacher-in-training. "Finish those peas first."

I tried to reason with him, but he was insistent. I cautioned him that I'd get sick if he forced me to eat them. He wouldn't budge, and so I dutifully shoveled the peas in, one sickening forkful at a time. Sure enough, those green peas and the rest of the dinner that had preceded them were soon all over the table in front of me. I hadn't been able to hold it down. The poor supervisor jumped out of his seat and came around to pat me on the back and apologize profusely. To this day, I won't touch a single green pea.

Classes at CID were small, mostly five to six students. In the early years, we stayed with one teacher for the full day, but in the last four years between fourth and eighth grades, we moved from classroom to classroom for reading, geography, arithmetic, social studies, and science. The teachers were excellent and very patient with us. All the teachers were hearing, and there were no interpreters since the main thrust of the school's pedagogical modality was oral education. Mrs. Skinner, who had taught my mother how to read, was my reading teacher as well.

I was always busy at school. For instance, there was the Goldstein Club (named after the school's founder, Max A. Goldstein, MD), which taught us how to run meetings using parliamentary procedures. We served on committees and became officers. I also learned how to appreciate parliamentary procedures, which, in my opinion, was all common sense and promoted fairness and respect for members' opinions. This basic level of experience influenced me later to become engaged in community activities and assume officer/leadership roles in various consumer and civic organizations.

I joined the Cub Scouts and then the Boy Scouts, where I earned merit badges and rose to the rank of patrol leader. We did a lot of projects and went on many outings, including swimming, knot tying, and overnight camping trips. My scoutmaster was Frank Withrow, who was also my woodworking teacher. He later earned his doctorate and held high positions in the US Department of Education and served as a project liaison officer for RIT/NTID and Gallaudet University. One March, I was somewhat mischievous and talked too much in a Boy Scouts meeting, and Mr. Withrow asked me to be quiet and behave. Arrogantly and carelessly, I ignored him and continued to talk with other scouts. Mr. Withrow came up to me and stripped my patrol leader stripes right from the sleeve of my shirt. I was dumbfounded and quickly shut up. That was that: I was no longer a patrol leader.

My summer months spent at home in Sioux City were nearly as busy as school, between visiting my grandparents and other relatives, reading with my mother, and playing and watching sports with my father. He'd happily play ball with me outside for hours at a time. Being a staunch sports fan, my father loved to read newspapers about sports and talk sports with his deaf friends and me. We went to watch the Sioux City Soos, a Class A farm team of the New York Giants, although the St. Louis Cardinals has always been my favorite team since I was a tot. I learned later that a Sioux City baseball team was one of the first farm teams of the St. Louis Cardinals in the 1920s, but it was dissolved, and later the New York Giants formed a new farm team, the Sioux City Soos, in the 1940s. This was an odd choice since the Cardinals received a lot of coverage in the Sioux City newspapers and radio/television stations.

My father and I also went to watch men play fast-pitch softball games at a field just a short drive from our home, close to where Dean Kruger, a close deaf family friend, lived. Dean and a few other deaf adults often went with us to watch the games, and we loved to talk about sports.

My mother read books to me every chance she got or retold me stories she'd recently read in a book. She was dedicated to sharing articles with me about successful deaf people in various professions. Her message was clear: You can accomplish great things. You can become whatever you want to become.

WHEN I RETURNED to school at CID that fall, Mr. Withrow asked me if I had learned my lesson, and I quickly replied that I had. Over the summer, I hadn't given much thought to my demotion, but I'd certainly absorbed that my insubordination had been wrong the moment he'd ripped the patrol leader stripes from my uniform. "Good," he said to my answer. "I'm going to reinstate your role as patrol leader then," and he handed me back the stripes. I learned from this incident an essential lesson about respect for adults, their responsibilities, and their authority. Perhaps more importantly, I also learned that people are capable of improving themselves if given another chance to prove themselves, especially if they are eager to learn and grow, as I was.

There was no harder worker than my father, but I saw that some-times, hard work didn't guarantee that you would move up a career ladder. After four years at the bakery, my father became ill, perhaps from the extreme heat of the ovens, and left the bakery. An old family friend who owned the Sioux City Furniture Company hired my father as an upholsterer.

My mother worked hard too. Once I started school in St. Louis, she worked to help pay for my tuition. My Uncle Bill (Mazie), my pa-ternal grandmother's half-brother, also helped pay for my education by way of an interest-free loan to my parents, who faithfully paid him back in small monthly installments for several years after I complet-ed my elementary education. Uncle Bill's generosity and my parents' commitment to paying him back taught me that it is important to pay it forward and to continuously be aware of other people who may not be as privileged.

Before each of my summer breaks from CID, my mother would ask her supervisor if she could take time off without pay so that she could be with me. Her request was denied every time, so she always quit her job, spent the summer taking care of me, and then searched for anoth-er job after I went back to school in the fall. Over the ten years I was at CID, she had ten different jobs doing manual labor, such as sewing, cleaning, and assembly-line work.

After I started junior high school, my mother decided to look for a permanent job. She had always wanted to work at Wincharger Ze-nith Radio. She had a keen knack for working with electronics; she figured out how to fix our old television and do other repairs around the house. She applied to Wincharger and, after not being contacted, she reapplied. She finally decided to go to the human resources office to apply in person, but they told her there was nothing for her.

My mother remained in the waiting room all day until the person-nel officer finally asked her to leave. My mother offered to work for free for the next two or three weeks. As a result of her assertiveness, the personnel officer told her to come to work the following Monday. She stayed at the job for the next twenty-five years working as a qual-ity control tester for radios on the assembly line. She was a valued em-ployee and received full retirement benefits. My mother's persistence and hard work taught me the value of being a conscientious employee,

Skippy and me.

and I have encouraged others to take their work seriously and always do the best possible job.

MY MOTHER HAD grown up with cats, and there was always a cat in our house in Sioux City. Betty was a black cat with one white foot. Socks was a brown and gray tabby with four white feet, thus the name. Blackie was a long-haired black cat who napped on a chair in the kitchen all day long. But when I was eleven years old, my parents got me a puppy, and I was thrilled. I named him Skippy. He was a rat terrier, white with a brown face and three large brown spots on his back. He was a strong, smart dog and loved to play with us and perform tricks. None of the cats had ever performed a single trick, as far as I could remember.

We were as close as brothers, Skippy and I, and I took him out every day for hour-long walks. One day, when we'd had Skippy for about eight years, I was sitting on the porch when a neighbor ran to let me know that Skippy had been run over by a car over on a nearby block. I sprinted to the car and found Skippy lying underneath the vehicle. The driver had tried to retrieve him, but Skippy had snapped and growled and refused to come out. But as soon as Skippy saw me, he crawled slowly, painfully toward me. It was obvious his back was broken. I picked him up as gently as I could and held him in my arms. "Let me take you to the veterinarian," the driver said, and so I sat in the back seat holding Skippy, who looked at me the whole time with sad eyes. The vet confirmed that his back was broken and couldn't be repaired. "We should put him down to end his suffering," the doctor advised me.

"Can I be alone with him first, for a minute?" I asked.

Sitting in the exam room, I petted my friend softly, trying to communicate through stroking the fur on his face and shoulders how much I loved him. After the doctor returned and put him down and he was gone, I was heartbroken, naturally, but also grateful that I had eight wonderful years with such a good dog.

ON THE LAST SABBATH before I would return to school for my last year at CID, my mother's childhood friend, Josephine Lynn, was visiting us from Kansas City. That night, she joined us at my grandparents' house for Shabbat dinner. On the short ride there, my mouth watered in anticipation because I knew my grandmother had been baking and cooking for the past two days in preparation, as she always did.

Sure enough, the table was laid with a white cloth, and there was challah bread and rugelach, meat-stuffed cabbage rolls, matzo ball soup, roasted chicken, and apple cake. My aunts and uncles, who sometimes just dropped by the house on Fridays to pick up baked goods grandmother had made for them, were this time staying for dinner too.

MY PATERNAL GRANDPARENTS were Orthodox Jews and religious-ly observed Sabbath every Friday evening and Saturday, along with all the Jewish holidays. My grandfather walked to United Orthodox Synagogue every Saturday morning, and often my father would join him; however, my grandfather had discouraged both my father and me from pursuing bar mitzvah because he believed that the Torah exempted individuals who did not possess all of their senses from this responsibility.

I attended the services with my father during the Jewish holidays, and sometimes my grandmother and my mother would join us. It was challenging and somewhat tedious because the services were conducted primarily in Hebrew, and there were no interpreters back then. Neither my parents nor I could read Hebrew, but many of the books had both English and Hebrew versions of the prayers, and we would pass the time reading the English pages of the prayer books.

That night at my grandparent's Shabbat dinner, my grandfather did a lot of praying in Hebrew, which the rest of us couldn't follow. We simply sat in silence and waited for him to finish before we could go on with the dinner, and conversation could start up again. When the initial prayers had been said over the bread and wine, and everyone was enjoying the delicious food and talking, for some reason my mother's friend Josephine, who was Catholic, reached down to get something from her purse. A little picture of Jesus fell out onto the floor between Josephine's chair and my grandfather's. We all held our breath while my grandfather picked it up from the floor and looked at it. After a few seconds, he said, "Jesus was a good man," and gave the picture back to Josephine, who slipped it quickly into her purse. We all breathed a sigh of relief.

CID ONLY WENT UP to eighth grade. In the weeks leading to my graduation, I was torn between excitement to be returning to Sioux City and my family, and sadness that the camaraderie and fun I'd experienced was coming to an end. In my ten years at CID, I'd grown independent, confident, interested in math and science and sports, mature, and happy to discover that I had some aptitude for leadership. And over those ten years, I'd been relatively unbothered by the discrimination or isolation that sometimes follows deaf people. I was fully confident that I would excel at home, just as I had in St. Louis.

While I felt ready to go into the public school's ninth grade, my mother had different ideas. When I returned home, she insisted that I repeat the eighth grade because she thought I needed time to adjust from the small classes at CID to the large classes that had all hearing students. She explained that I didn't know anyone from my neighborhood who was going to the same school, didn't have any brothers or sisters to share experiences with me or give me support, and didn't really have any friends in Sioux City. We argued hotly, but my mother stood by her decision. She told me that Dr. Helen S. Lane, the principal at CID, supported her decision, and that was that.

4

Public School in Sioux City

I LIKED MY blue-and-brown plaid shirt—it looked good on me. I checked my hair one last time in the bathroom mirror then did an about-face and headed to the front door. My mother was there to wish me good luck. I grabbed my book bag, which already held five textbooks, even though it was just the first day of school—eighth grade at North Junior High. In the weeks leading up to school, we'd gone together to the school to sign me up, introduce me to the principal, and get some of the course materials. I would be the only deaf student in my class of several hundred boys and girls.

The school was within walking distance from home, and I set off into the crisp September morning. Home at last. Public school. This was really a new phase of life I was entering, and it was going to be a great one, I was sure. I'd always loved school, and now I'd have the fun and excitement of school combined with the comforts of home and the pleasure of being with my family every day, not just on holidays and over the summer.

When I neared the school's entrance, the front of the school was crowded with kids my age swarming up the steps. Inside, the blue-tiled hallways were crowded too. What were people saying? Greeting each other, comparing schedules, and saying things I couldn't quite catch. People brushed by as I checked my schedule, which I'd folded

neatly and put into my front pocket. First period was US history, with
Mrs. Poppin, in room 48.

Mrs. Poppin, an elderly teacher with short, graying black hair and
a friendly smile, seemed to recognize me as a new student right away.
"Welcome to class!" she said and led me to a seat in the third row,
near the front. When everyone had taken their seats, she announced
my presence, saying, "Boys and girls, we have a new student joining
us today, Tracy Hurwitz, and I'd like you to make him feel very welcome. Tracy is from right here in Sioux City, but he has been attending a school for the deaf in St. Louis." Out of the corner of my eye, I
saw ten heads turn to look at me. The students in the rows ahead of
mine twisted in their seats to glance back at me. There were at least
forty students in the class, with desks extending to the very back of
the room. I imagined that everyone behind me was now looking at the
back of my blue-and-brown checked shirt.

Should I turn now and wave at my classmates behind me? I decided against it. I hoped Mrs. Poppin would change the subject fast, to
something about US history as soon as possible, and thankfully, she
did. It took all my concentration to follow what she was saying. I
missed what my classmates were saying back to her. If only we could
be seated in a big circle, where I could see everyone at once!

Later, I noticed that all my classmates to my left and right and in
the seats in front of me had pulled out their heavy textbooks and
opened them to the same page. There was an illustration of Abraham
Lincoln standing at a podium in a field, flanked by other dark-coat-
ed speakers to his left and right. Mrs. Poppin caught my eye as she
was speaking. She was saying something about reciting aloud. Did she
want me to? But no, not just me. I saw that all my classmates were
reading in unison from the textbook now: ". . . brought forth upon
this continent a new nation, conceived in liberty and dedicated to the
proposition that all men are created equal . . ." I flipped through the
book and found the page and quickly scanned the Gettysburg Address printed there for the correct section, to match my classmates. It
was a delicate maneuver, like landing a plane in a windstorm, but by
glancing up at the boy one row ahead of mine and on the aisle, noting
what he was saying, and then glancing down quickly at the text, I was
able to determine the right part of the address to come in on. "It is

At age thirteen.

altogether fitting and proper that we should do this." And then I continued to the next paragraph, my voice as clear and strong, I hoped, as my classmates' voices. "But, in a larger sense, we can not dedicate—we can not consecrate—we can not hallow—this ground. The brave men, living and dead, who struggled here, have consecrated it far above our power to add or detract. The world will little note, nor long remember, what we say here, but it can never forget what they did here." Head down, eyes concentrating on the words, I was reading steadily for a while before something made me glance up. Mrs. Poppin was smiling kindly, directly at me, and some of my classmates were staring at me, some were smirking. "Please, do continue, Tracy," Mrs. Poppin said encouragingly. I had been reading aloud alone, somehow missing the cue to stop. Maybe she had told the class to read up until a certain line, and I had missed that instruction. I wanted to find a hole in the floor and disappear. But, as usual in these situations, there was no boy-sized hole conveniently located nearby, and so I suffered through the rest of the class, my humiliation making my face hot. When it was time to go to the next class—all my classmates started gathering their things, or they leaped straight from their chairs and headed to the door—I realized I didn't know if we had homework or not. I'd have to check with the teacher.

"Do we have homework?" I asked Mrs. Poppin.

"Excuse me, Tracy?" she said. She hadn't understood me.

"Do we have homework?" I had to ask her several times before she understood my question.

Walking to my next class, I vowed to survive it without any further humiliating moments. My mind went back to CID, where I could understand exactly what was going on in every class, where my classmates were more like siblings than strangers, where I knew every nook and cranny, every side door, every sidewalk and windowpane by heart. At CID, I'd been an excellent and popular student. At CID, it had always been easy for us to jump into conversations with our teachers and classmates since we understood each other, and the class sizes were small.

In my first few months at North Junior High, I often didn't understand homework assignments or what to do on a test. In social studies, I went to the teacher on several consecutive days to ask him if I had done my work correctly. He finally got impatient with me and wrote down on a piece of paper, "Do you want to be spoon-fed all the time?" I was puzzled. What did that mean, "spoon-fed?" I didn't know, but what was clear was that he didn't want to answer my question. I walked back to my seat with a sheepish smile. That was the last time I asked him for feedback.

At least on the playing field, I knew what was happening, and I could excel. Before school started, a bunch of boys played football or baseball in the large park across the street from the school. If I left the house by 6:45, I'd get to the park by 7:00, an hour before school started at 8:00—enough time to play a whole football game or a few innings of baseball.

My favorite sport, though, was basketball. I decided to try out for the school's team. The day after the first tryout, the coach posted a sheet on the wall outside the gymnasium with the names of those who'd made the cut. My name was there! I went to another tryout, and again my name appeared on the list. I survived three cuts before my name no longer appeared on the list. I didn't understand why, but

I didn't talk with the coach. It was not until I was a junior at Central High School that I realized I needed to go to all the tryout sessions in order for the coach to continue to evaluate my athletic skills. I didn't know about this requirement since I had no previous experience in trying out for athletic teams at school. I might have missed an announcement or didn't understand the coach when he was talking to us during tryout sessions. Nobody else asked me about it, so I simply waited for a final decision. Then it was too late, and by then, I had already blown out my left knee after playing football in a community league, so I never had a chance to join the high school basketball team. I did join the JV golf team, though. I also tried out for swimming and track, but I didn't have the stamina for distance trials. Mostly, I played softball and basketball for community leagues at the Jewish Community Center in the evenings and on weekends and during the summers. Many days, when I walked into the house after school, my mother would be sitting at the kitchen table reading a copy of her favorite publication, The Silent Worker, which in 1966 would change its name to The Deaf American. Published by the National Association for the Deaf (NAD), the magazine was a rich source of news and of happenings that didn't quite qualify as news: "Jake Roberts of Minneapolis is set to retire on Jan. 1, but he admits recently that his plans may go awry unless his boss is able to find a man to take his place as a cylinder pressman for the American Printing Co. He specializes in color posters. For the past year or so, he has been suffering from a heart ailment and anemia." This window into the lives of deaf people around the country, long before captioned television or the internet or even TTY (teletypewriter), gave us an idea of what was possible. The magazine also offered inspiring biographical profiles of deaf people, speeches and letters by prominent deaf Americans, meeting minutes from NAD's annual convention, and essays and speeches by Gallaudet University presidents.

"There's a deaf man from Sioux Falls," my mother told me, "who moved up to Alaska with almost no money in his pocket in 1939, and today, he is one of the most successful hunters in Alaska! He owns several houses and is about to retire from the Alaska Road Commission!" My mother showed me the article, which had three photos. One was of Jonah Ephraim Evans in the snow on a sled pulled by a dozen dogs. Another was of his ramshackle hunting cabin that *The*

Silent Worker claimed was one of the finest in all of Alaska, partly because it was so well situated to store lots of animal meat. The last photograph was of Evans holding a rifle proudly and leaning up against the first moose he'd ever shot, a mammoth animal that weighed nearly 1,000 pounds and whose antlers spanned fifty-four inches.

"See?" my mother said. "You can be whatever you want to be."

All I wanted to be right then was a happy and successful junior high school student, but it was turning out to be much harder than I'd anticipated. In math class that week, as the teacher was writing out a mathematical formula, I noticed a mistake in the computation he'd written on the blackboard. Now *here* was a chance to participate! I'd always excelled at math, and math was a very precise language, for all its complexity. Either something was correct, or it wasn't. If I pointed out the error, I would demonstrate to the teacher my understanding of the concept we were covering in trigonometry, and I'd also be joining in on the conversation, something I found difficult to do. I raised my hand.

"Sir, there is a mistake in the computation," I said.

"What's that? What did you say, Tracy?" the teacher asked.

I repeated myself three or four more times, but he couldn't understand me. My speech was not always intelligible to hearing people who were not accustomed to listening to deaf people who used their voice. OK, I thought, I'll just walk up to the board to make the correction myself. That will clear up all confusion. But, as I got closer to the board, I realized that the teacher was right. There was no error to correct! And here I was, at the front of the class, with every eye on me and the teacher looking at me with great interest and confusion, and possibly some irritation at the interruption. How I wished I hadn't opened my mouth! Once again—this was becoming a theme for me at this school—I wanted to vanish. Instead, I walked nonchalantly back to my seat, in the manner of James Dean walking in *Rebel without a Cause*. As I slid back into my chair, I said, "Never mind." I don't think the teacher ever understood what I was talking about.

When my second report card arrived in the mail that year, it was like the first one had been: a disaster. I got Ds in all of my courses, except for gym, which I got an A for. My mother was worried, but not very surprised. She'd known the transition would be hard. Not only were my grades poor, but most of my interactions with teachers and classmates were fleeting and superficial—one-on-one exchanges outside of the classroom; some of them could understand my speech, but mostly I'd have to repeat myself more than once. My classmates and I would greet each other and talk a little about the weather, sports, cars, and school. We did not have deep and meaningful conversations. At times, we'd resort to writing on paper or a blackboard. My mother had been right: I was not prepared for a mainstreamed experience after spending ten years in self-contained, small classes at CID. Something would have to change.

OUR NEIGHBORS ACROSS the street had a son, Gary, who was three years older than me. While I'd been away at school, Gary had gotten to know my parents. He seemed fascinated by them and loved talking with them. When I'd come home for holidays and over the summer, Gary and I would sometimes talk on the sidewalks outside our houses, and over time, we'd become friends. Gary was into music and was a member of the high school drum corps. He was a fun and amusing friend who loved to laugh. We'd sit on the curb of busy streets near our neighborhood and name each vehicle that passed by us. "1941 Pontiac Streamliner," "1949 Ford Club Coupe," or, "1955 Ford Fairlane." We could tell the year, make, and model of all the cars manufactured in the late 1940s and the 1950s. "Imagine driving up to the high school in a blue Cadillac El Dorado," Gary said. "Or," I countered, "a white Chrysler Windsor, top down." We could picture our friends' and neighbors' surprised and impressed expressions. Everyone would be dazzled by our good taste.

Gary's favorite celebrity was Pat Boone, a pop singer second in popularity at the time only to *my* idol, Elvis Presley. Gary and I loved to impersonate famous entertainers and musicians, especially Boone and Elvis. I combed my long hair into a ducktail, rolled up my short-sleeved shirts, and flipped my collar up. I didn't smoke, so I didn't have a cigarette packet in my sleeve, but I wore black motorcycle boots with a buckle on each boot. One day, Gary and I were hanging out together at a park, and a big group of guys from the high school joined us. After a while, the two of us headed back to our block, and Gary said, "You sure are lucky you're deaf!"

"What do you mean?" I asked him.

Gary said that other boys were making dirty and nasty remarks about my being deaf.

"What did they say?" I asked.

"Never mind," Gary said. "They were just not being nice about deaf people." I shrugged, not wanting Gary to know that this news bothered me. I'd thought those were nice boys, and I'd thought they understood that I was just as smart, just as capable, as they were. But I'd been mistaken. People had many misconceptions about being deaf and what a deaf person could do, maybe misconceptions about what deaf people thought about and hoped for. Deaf people can become hunters in Alaska, teachers, investors, artists, I thought of saying. But I kept my cool on the rest of the walk home.

From that day, it became important for me to educate the public that deaf people could do anything they aspired to do. I couldn't keep getting Ds in school, that was for sure. In ninth grade, I made an effort to get to know the teachers at school better. I went to the public library many times every week and studied concepts and material the teachers had covered in class.

My new tactics paid off. I did better. The math teacher even posted my tests on the bulletin board when I got a perfect score. He told the class, "If Tracy, being deaf, can do this well, then everyone else in the class can do better too."

One day in ninth grade, though, I was drinking water from a low-level fountain in a hallway when someone pushed my head down into the stream of water, causing my face to be all wet. I looked up in surprise and saw a guy in my class standing above me, laughing. It caught me by surprise. Since I was not a fighter or a rebellious guy, I decided not to do anything and instead laughed with him. A few days later, he must have realized he had been wrong. He came up to me in the hall and said he was sorry for what he did to me. I accepted his apology and, by getting to know each other through working on school projects together, we became good friends and even joined the Boy Scouts together. He eventually went to and graduated from West Point.

My tenure in the Boy Scouts in Sioux City did not last long since the scoutmaster moved out of town within months, and the troop was disbanded. I rose up close to Life Star but never had a chance to become an Eagle Scout. This is one goal I still regret not having achieved during my journey.

After ninth grade, I attended Central High School and did well academically, although interpreters or support/access services continued to be nonexistent. I obviously did not learn very much in the classroom because I could not always understand the teachers or my classmates. I met with teachers after class to find out about homework assignments. I continued to visit the public library almost every night to look for additional information so that I could keep up with my schoolwork.

5

A Good Day's Work

My friend Gary would soon be graduating from high school and leaving for his work life. "You could take over my paper route," he told me one day. "It's fun, and it's pretty good money."

He was right. I woke at 4:30 each morning to walk a little more than a mile to pick up the papers, fold each into four parts in a square, stuff them into two bags over my shoulders, and deliver them to approximately seventy-five customers. Sometimes in good weather, I'd ride my bike and deliver papers while riding. I'd hurl the folded papers onto porches from where I was on the sidewalk. Most of the time, my aim was accurate; other times, I'd miss my target, and occasionally accidentally throw the newspaper onto the roof. When that happened, I would walk up to the house and take the folded papers out from my bag, tie two bags together, and swirl them above my head to swipe the newspaper back to the ground. There was one house where a beautiful and friendly dog, a boxer, would come running at me so that I'd place the paper directly in its mouth. He'd then run back to his master standing on the porch. After I completed my circuit by 6 a.m., I walked back home to clean up, eat breakfast, and then walk another mile to school.

Another dog on my route, a vicious-looking brown dog, possibly a cross between a German Shepherd and a bulldog, once burst out of the bushes flanking a blue house and barreled toward me, his teeth

Collecting a subscription payment from one of my favorite customers.

showing and his jaws working as he barked like mad. I was ready for him. I lifted one of the bags from my shoulder and began swinging it in the air, faster and faster. Before he reached me, the dog veered off his course to avoid being hit. I kept the bag swinging, and the dog trotted back into his yard, where he continued to bark at me, but with less ferocity.

On Thursday and Friday evenings, I went to each customer's home to collect money, using a hole-puncher to validate the weekly payment on their tickets. A few customers were delinquent in their weekly payments, so I'd keep going after them to pay up. Other customers would pay several weeks in advance, and I was careful not to overspend my weekly earnings so I could put aside the money for the following weeks. One customer—a very sweet ninety-year-old lady—always invited me into the house for a glass of milk and cookies and a short chat. Mostly, we talked about the weather and my schooling. She also showed me pictures of her family.

Every Saturday morning, I went to the newspaper office to turn in the payments, and I kept a weekly profit of about twelve dollars.

For nearly two years during high school, I also worked at a drive-in car wash two hours per day after school and on weekends when I could. It was an interesting experience, especially driving fancy cars into and out of the automated car wash and cleaning up the insides. Most of the young workers were high school dropouts, alcoholics, or drug users. Many came from broken homes, and they often showed up at work with a black eye or some other injury from fights. I got along with my car wash colleagues, though I didn't hang around with them outside of work.

IF I MADE THIS SHOT, I'd win because we were playing to twenty-two points. I pivoted, dribbled twice to my friend Dennis's side. then went up for the jump shot inside the foul line. It bounced off the rim, and Dennis leaped up and got the rebound. He was taller than me, so he often beat me at our one-on-one games, but I was determined to beat him this time. I reached in and grabbed the ball before he could shoot. He grinned and started to crowd me, saying something about fouls. This was a good time for a hook shot. I went for it, picturing the correct arc of the ball as it left my hand. Two points!

On our walk home, Dennis said he was thinking of joining the military. "You should," I told him.

Where would my place be in society, in the workforce? I wondered. Not in the military probably. I didn't think the Army allowed deaf men to serve. My mother's magazine stories told me that I could do almost anything. My father and his deaf friends' examples showed, in contrast, that I would most likely work with my hands.

My summer job throughout high school was working as an upholsterer with my father at Sioux City Furniture Company, housed on the ground floor of a three-story brick building with cement floors, small windows high up on the wall, and no air-conditioning. Temperatures in the factory often reached a stifling 90 degrees Fahrenheit in the summer. I worked on an assembly line where carts piled with furniture rolled by on a conveyor belt. Every worker on the line had a specific assignment, such as putting together woodwork and springs, stuffing in cotton, and hammering nails into the coverings. We'd rotate roles so that we all were familiar with the entire furniture-making process.

During my third summer at the furniture company, they introduced a new technology: a hydraulic air gun that pushed nails into the coverings that draped over the wooden furniture frames rather than manually hammering individual nails in one by one. I had developed a trick of picking up a handful of magnetic nails and putting them in my mouth, then using the magnetic hammer to draw out a nail from my mouth and hammer it into the furniture. It took a lot of skill to do this rhythmically. One afternoon, I somehow managed to swallow a nail. I turned off the magnetic hammer, put it down, and ran to the part of the factory floor where my father was sanding wood.

"Dad!" I said. "I swallowed a nail! What should I do?"

He laughed. "Nothing. It will come out at the other end," he told me with an air of unconcern that I felt was at odds with the severity of the situation.

I never saw it come out, but I didn't really want to know where it went.

Another time, I accidentally cut my left forefinger with a sharp curved knife while cutting cardboard. A massive amount of blood gushed out, and my father casually told me to stick my finger in a pail of turpentine. I plunged my finger into the oil, and miraculously, the bleeding stopped immediately, but the flesh was burned off my finger. I was amazed at this sight. That experience inspired me to be more careful, as I didn't want to experience turpentine-dunking ever again.

Wasn't there somewhere better to work than with my father? During the summer before my senior year, I wanted a different experience. I talked with one of my parents' close deaf friends, Dean Kruger, who was a master cabinetmaker for another company. He also had a private cabinet-making business at home. He talked with his boss, who agreed to hire me as an apprentice cabinetmaker. Like the furniture company where my father and I worked, this plant was not air-conditioned, but I enjoyed interacting with my wonderful coworkers there. One time, during a break, I declared to a coworker that I was not interested in getting married until I was thirty-five or older.

"Well," he said, smiling knowingly, "if the right girl comes along, you shouldn't waste time though!" I laughed, thinking he was kidding. The idea of getting married young was just plain funny to me.

That Monday, my supervisor at the cabinet-making company explained that my task for the day was to sand small pieces of wood until they were completely smooth. He handed me one to start with. "Get that smooth, and then call me over, and I'll check your work," he told me. Following instructions, I started with the coarsest sandpaper, then worked my way down to the finer-grained paper, trying as best as I could to keep the strokes in line with the woodgrain. When it was as smooth as I could get it, I brought it over to the boss to inspect. He turned it over in his hands a few times and then looked up at me with a frown. "Not yet!" he said. "Give it another try, son." Over and over, I tried to get it smoother, brought it to the supervisor to check, and was sent back to try again.

That night, I lay in bed, marveling at how I could try my best at something—something seemingly so simple—and still not succeed. I flipped my pillow over to have the cool side against my cheek, and the flipping reminded me of flipping that small piece of wood I'd had to sand smooth. In my dreams, I sanded and sanded my car, but it stubbornly refused to become a motorcycle. When I washed my face the next morning, I noted how smooth the bar of soap was in my hands, and how the water rushing over it from the faucet would eventually melt it away to nothing, without effort.

After about three more weeks of working at Dean Kruger's cabinet-making factory, I received a pink slip thanking me for my service and saying that I was no longer needed. However, I did get paid for my final week of forty hours. "I am good at some things and not so good at other things," I realized. Now the idea of college took on new urgency for me.

Back then, there were only two viable jobs that a deaf person could expect to have: a Linotype operator/printer or teacher. Yes, there were other jobs available, such as upholsterer, cabinetmaker, farmer, and factory worker. But I wasn't interested in any of those.

Some deaf people were regular peddlers, and I was friendly with them. A common choice of peddled goods was a card showing the manual alphabet in sign language, and the peddlers traveled all over the country selling them. Other peddlers would make things—knitted items, wood carvings, quilted potholders, pipes. Many paid their taxes, but the ones who peddled the ABC cards often avoided doing so. I realized later that they enjoyed selling things, and when they couldn't get jobs as salespeople, they went into peddling. I knew that I would not be good at sales.

Being a Linotype operator or working in a printing company had its advantages. Most employees were members of the International Typographical Union (ITU, the union for Linotype printers, typesetters, and press operators), which allowed them to travel anywhere in the country and work for any newspaper or printing company that hired ITU members. It was an attractive job for many deaf people who learned the skills in high school, and they certainly made a good living. Unfortunately, the field drastically changed when computers began to emerge, and so-called "hot type" printing transformed into "cold type" digital typesetting. Many deaf people who were members of the ITU left the printing industry and moved on to computer-related jobs that no longer offered union membership.

Teaching was another viable option, but it required a college education and would mean going to Gallaudet College for teacher preparation. I did think about becoming a teacher, but my mother discouraged me from pursuing a teaching degree. When I tried to dispute her views, she decided I should meet with an elderly deaf teacher who'd graduated from Gallaudet, to hear about his teaching experience. My parents drove me to my father's alma mater, ISD in Council Bluffs, to meet with him. "Forget it," he told me, regarding a future in teaching. I was surprised and disappointed by his response. He explained that teaching was not a good future for deaf people because there would be no opportunities for advancement. He had remained at the same level for many years and had to first work as a houseparent in the dormitory. The conversation was enough to convince me to put teaching in the back of my mind and instead explore other careers. I thought about becoming a lawyer or even a veterinarian but was told by others that deaf people couldn't pursue these fields since strong oral communication skills and the ability to hear were required.

My favorite uncle was Max Ellis, who was married to my father's sister, Aunt Cranie. Max and Cranie lived in Cleveland, and we were planning a visit.

"Maybe your Uncle Max will show you where he works," my mother suggested. It was a good idea. Uncle Max was a deaf man with a good job, and he and Aunt Cranie seemed to have a good life. They lived in a pretty apartment in a pleasant suburb, and Uncle Max always seemed happy and relaxed. He loved to talk about his work as a draftsman for Bailey Meter, a manufacturer of industrial control systems and equipment. I doubted that he had to work in 90-degree heat with no breeze to relieve the swelter.

My guess was correct. He gave me a private tour of Bailey Meter, which also had offices in Buffalo, Cincinnati, and Pittsburgh. The place was clean, well lit, and air-conditioned.

"I'd like you to meet my nephew Tracy," Uncle Max said, introducing me to his supervisor and coworkers, who all nodded and smiled and shook my hand. Uncle Max's drafting table was large and angled and filled with fancy drawing tools. He then took me around the plant to show me where the meters were manufactured. By the time we'd seen it all and were ready to leave him to his work, I had made up my mind. I would become a draftsman like him!

A few weeks later, in my junior year of high school, Mr. Ray Obermiller, also known as Coach Obermiller, called me into his office to talk about my future. He was the guidance counselor.

"What are your plans after high school, Tracy?" he asked me.

"I want to be a draftsman," I told him.

"Why is that?" he asked, somewhat to my surprise. I told him about Uncle Max's work and my tour of his office and the factory.

"That does sound like a possibility," Coach agreed, "But I think you could go to a four-year college."

Drafting required only a few months of training in a vocational school, not four years of college, I knew.

"What kind of job are you thinking of?" I asked him.

"Have you ever thought about engineering?"

I pictured a train chugging through the prairie, big plumes of coal smoke puffing out of its chimney. "Do you mean a train engineer?" I asked.

"No, I mean engineering, a higher form of analytical and design work that requires extensive college-level coursework in mathematics and science. You've done well in all of your college preparatory courses—English, math, and science—so you should seriously think about going to college."

That got me thinking. I discussed it with Uncle Max during his next visit to Sioux City to find out what he thought about my going into engineering. He was astonished and said it would require many years of study and that it would be a very difficult major. He never thought a deaf person could become an engineer since he did not know of any. He explained that as a draftsman, he worked closely with a team of engineers who gave him instructions to do his work and that engineers must work with a lot of hearing people inside and outside the company. I realized that if it was going to be a challenge, then that's what I wanted to do.

In my later years as a professional, I worked with young deaf college students who wanted to become engineers or computer scientists. I recognized that it was crucial for younger students to be exposed to career opportunities as early as possible. I asked the dean of the engineering college at RIT how early a student should learn more about an engineering career to be better prepared for a rigorous engineering education in college. Like Mr. Obermiller, the dean said that it was important for young students to start preparing as early as seventh grade or even earlier so that they could take four years each of high school math, science, and, of course, English. He believed that with solid college preparatory courses in high school, students would be better prepared for anything—including science, technology, engineering, and mathematics—in college. After that, I made it a mission in my professional life to encourage students, families, and teachers to commit to preparing young deaf and hard of hearing students for advanced education in high school and college.

Once I decided I wanted to be an engineer, I sent out requests for information from many different colleges and universities. I was appalled when I got the packets from them addressing me as Miss Tracy Hurwitz. This was in the early 1960s, and it bothered me a great deal. I complained to my mother, who told me to disregard it. I wrote back to some of the colleges and stressed that my name was Tracy *Alan* Hurwitz; still, I got responses from them addressing me as Miss Tracy Alan Hurwitz. I became more infuriated and responded with my name as Mr. Tracy Alan Hurwitz. The problem never got resolved so I tried my best to live with it.

6

Love at Second Sight

IN MY FOURTH YEAR as a newspaper delivery boy, I received a scholarship from the *Sioux City Journal* to attend Morningside College, a local four-year liberal arts college. It was a recognition of my successful years on the route as well as my academic record.

A reporter came to the house to interview me. He asked about my high school classes, my career ambitions, my dedicated paper delivery, and the highs and lows of delivering the paper.

"This is great, thank you," he told me after we'd spoken for about twenty minutes. "My story about you should be in the paper next Sunday."

Close to midnight on Saturday, our doorbell rang. This caused a series of lights to flash throughout the house, which woke us all up. My father pulled on his robe and rushed to the door, and I was not far behind him. Bob Dunnington, a deaf friend of my parents, stood on the doorstep. Bob worked as a Linotype operator at the *Journal,* and he wanted to alert me that the article was hitting the presses with the title, "Deaf Mute Successful on a Route."

Mute? I wasn't mute! I was shocked and thanked Bob for letting us know.

I grabbed a dictionary, jumped into my car, and drove to the *Journal.* I looked around for the night editor and found him, a balding man in his fifties getting the paper ready for printing. I pushed the open dictionary toward him, pointing to the word *mute*. I read the definition aloud to him: "speechless or unable to think."

"Oh, gosh!" he said, pushing his glasses up on his head and rubbing his eyes. He looked up at me, embarrassed. "I'm so sorry, son! How about we change 'mute' to 'dumb?'"

"That's worse!" I said, flipping as quickly as I could to the "D" section of the dictionary. "Here," I said, showing him that "dumb" was defined as "speechless and unintelligent."

He was dumbfounded and seemingly stumped. He tapped his front teeth with his index finger, squinting his eyes. "Well," he said at last, "I'll think of a better way to describe you."

I stood there wondering if I could trust him to come up with a better title since he had already suggested two inappropriate words. I decided to hope for the best, and I thanked him and left. The first thing the next morning, with something like dread, I looked for the article in our newspaper. There it was, accompanied by a large picture of me wearing my winter coat and standing with my favorite customer, the ninety-year-old lady, at her door: "Journal Boy Not Bothered by Handicap." Phew! Disaster averted. (Today, many decades later, we do not use the word *handicap* to describe deaf people and other people with disabilities; at the time, however, I was just happy not to be described as "dumb.")

Since I already had a scholarship from the *Sioux City Journal* to attend Morningside College in Sioux City, I decided to apply there. After I was accepted, I met with the registrar to prepare for my entry into the preengineering program that had a 2+3 arrangement with the Iowa State University School of Engineering in Ames. This program would allow me to study preengineering at Morningside for the first two years and then transfer to Iowa State for the last three years, enabling me to earn two degrees: a bachelor's in mathematics from Morningside and a bachelor of science degree in electrical engineering from Iowa State. Nice deal!

I tried to talk my friend Dennis into coming to Morningside with me.

"It'll be fun. It's a good school. It's coed!" I told him. But he had no interest in going to college, any college.

"I might join the Navy," Dennis told me. The military had been his idea all that year. I encouraged him to sign up, and one day that summer, he informed me that he'd applied and been accepted by the Navy.

"I'll get to see the world," he joked, "but unlike in the Army, I won't have to walk the whole way." He was supposed to get on the bus to the naval training academy in the middle of June, but he backed out at the last minute. His new enlistment date was set for July, but again, he backed out of getting on the bus at the last minute.

In August, a few weeks before I was to leave for Morningside, I told Dennis, "You've got to do it! Hey, I'll drive you myself." We packed his stuff into my car and drove him down to the bus depot. We hugged. I watched him hand over his suitcase to the driver to put under the bus and then walk up the stairs to take a window seat. He gave me a goofy smile—half-excited, half-scared. He waved. I waved. I waited until the bus pulled out of the lot and disappeared around the corner. I was relieved he was finally on his way.

THE SUMMER OF 1961, after my high school graduation, with Morningside College firmly in my future, the world looked bright. I'd faced the challenge of public school with hearing students and hearing teachers, and I'd prevailed. By taking my education into my own hands, working the extra hours in the library, and building relationships with my teachers and some of my classmates and neighbors, I'd come out of that bad place, where I was alone, confused, and failing. I had worked many jobs and earned and saved enough money to buy myself no fewer than three cars since turning sixteen. And I'd chosen a career path.

Since my mother was also an alumna, she had come with me to St. Louis for my first CID reunion, but she was staying with one of her old friends, while I was sharing a hotel room with my classmate, Bill, from Georgia. I was happy to see my old friends whom I hadn't seen for five years. We talked about our experiences in high school, and some of them (those who hadn't repeated eighth grade as I had) told the rest of us about their first year in college.

Bill and I, along with our classmate Karl, walked into the Roosevelt Hotel for lunch. The hotel's café featured a 1950s fountain-type counter with stools, and right away, I spied four other CID alums sitting in a booth. They were about the same age as us. One of them, a girl named Vicki, turned to see us walk in, and she said "Hi" to us. I shyly said "Hi" back, and turned around to sit at the counter and order my lunch.

After they were done with lunch, Vicki stopped next to me on their way out. "Do you remember me?" she asked.

"Yeah, I do," I said, and then, because I couldn't think of anything good to say next, went back to eating my lunch. Vicki and her friends walked away.

I did remember her from school. She'd been a little girl, about eight years old the last time I'd seen her. I remembered that she did solo dancing on the stage at CID. She was a good and graceful dancer and a cute and pretty girl, but I hadn't cared much for her at CID. I remembered her as always talking and telling others what to do, and I thought she was somewhat bossy. But at the café, I was surprised to see that she had become a beautiful young lady with a great personality. She must still be in high school, I realized.

Later that evening, another friend and I, late going to an alumni event on the four-level *Admiral* steamboat on the Mississippi River, raced through red lights in his car, speeding down empty streets near the river. It was sheer luck that he didn't get any traffic tickets. We screeched abruptly into a parking space by the pier and jumped out of the car. The crew was pulling up the ramp to the boat but waited a moment when they saw us, two desperate teens, rushing toward them.

We hadn't had time to eat dinner before getting on the boat, and I was hungry, so I went to get two hot dogs with all the trimmings. As I walked down the stairs to join the alumni group, Vicki happened to walk by. She gave me a small smile, and I smiled back and stopped to talk with her. She glanced meaningfully at my hot dogs and asked, "Are you hungry?"

"Yes!" I said. We could read each other's lips easily, which was very helpful, given that I was carrying hot dogs in both hands and Vicki didn't know "sign language" as we called it in those days. We talked while we walked until we joined our classmates, and then we sat next to each other and continued to chat away the rest of the evening. Later in the evening, I noticed that Vicki was cold, and so I gave her my jacket to cover her shoulders. We felt that we could talk together forever. Our eyes kept meeting, and when they did, it felt warm and exciting and right.

Back on land the next day, another alumnus came up to me and said, "Leave Vicki alone. She's my girlfriend, so back off." My reaction to his order surprised me. I felt not an inkling of backing off. "I don't know that," I told him with a shrug. He wanted to fight with me, so I said, "Fine, let's go outside." He decided to back off and left.

Vicki found out about our near skirmish from one of her friends and was furious at the other guy. She told him off, saying she was neither his girlfriend nor his property. Vicki was only seventeen but clearly had the maturity to handle it. I didn't know she knew what happened until she told me years later.

That same day, we all got on buses to go to Grant's Farm, an old St. Louis landmark and home to many different animals, including the famed Budweiser horses, for an all-day alumni event. I was on one bus and Vicki was on the other. After we got off the buses, I looked for her and found her, and when I ran into my mother, I introduced them to each other.

After a full day, we went back to our assigned buses, where my former classmate, Steve, from Ottawa, Canada, and I sat together. He was dating an alumna from Minnesota who was staying with Vicki at her home in St. Louis and was with her on the other bus. As we waited on the parked bus, looking out the window at the other bus, I asked Steve whether Vicki was dating anyone. When he asked me why I said I wanted to ask her to be my date to the banquet on the last night of the reunion. Steve jumped off the bus and ran to the next bus where Vicki was. As that bus began to pull away, Steve jumped back off of it and ran back to ours. He plunked himself down in his seat beside me, grinning. He'd asked Vicki point-blank if she was committed to anyone, he said, and Vicki had, without hesitation, replied, "No way!" and asked why. "I told her you wanted to ask her to go to the banquet with you, and Vicki said, 'Tell him YES!'" I was flattered; boy, did it feel good.

We got off the buses at an alumnus's home for a barbecue. Vicki saw my mother and told her that I had just asked her to the banquet. My mother was thrilled about this and chatted with Vicki for a bit.

The next day, Vicki and I decided to walk around Forest Park across the street from CID. As we walked, we talked a lot and eventually sat on a bench with a great view of a large pond glittering in the sun. Several groups of ducks and two large swans swam in little clusters on the surface of the water. Before we knew it, we kissed each other. We suddenly noticed a few alumni walking on the other side of the pond quite a distance away from us. We smiled but continued chatting.

"What time will you pick me up?" she asked, referring to the next evening's banquet.

"4:00 p.m. and I'll be riding on a motorcycle and wearing my leather jacket," I said. At first, she thought that I was serious.

That night, there was another alumni event at a bowling alley. Vicki and I had fun bowling and talking. She was so beautiful in her yellow dress. We decided to walk outside to the back of the building, where we passionately kissed each other. A short time later, we walked back to the front, and Vicki was petrified to see her father. His face was red with anger, and he was waiting to take her home. He commanded Vicki to get into the car, and as they drove off, I thought I was doomed. To my relief, she was still full of life the next day, and we continued to spend time together. I learned later that her father was more protective of Vicki than of his two younger, hearing daughters. Vicki's mother, on the other hand, was happy because she remembered seeing my picture and reading about my interview with the newspaper in the *CID Newsnotes*.

BEFORE I WENT TO COLLEGE, one of my last jobs was chasing turkeys. It was a one-time all-night job that some of my friends asked me to join them in doing. We were in the back of a pickup truck. The sun was sinking below the flat horizon, all orange and gold. I was glad I'd thought to wear my denim jacket because it was windy in the back of the truck. We laughed at the hair whipping into our eyes. The truck slowed and turned into a dirt driveway. We had arrived at the turkey farm. The farmer told us what to do, and it sounded pretty simple: "Go out to the field, catch turkeys, and when you catch one, bring it to this fenced area to be vaccinated. Then, dump the ones that have been vaccinated into this other fenced area."

Farmed turkeys are not that hard to catch (they can't fly), but it does take some scrambling, some sprinting. They can lay their necks down, point their heads forward, and race, their heads bobbing forward and back with each step. You had to set your sights on one, then go for it. The hardest part is after you've already gotten your hands around a turkey. The turkeys fought us with strong legs and sharp toenails. The best thing to do was hold it by its body out far away from your body as you carried it to the corral. We repeated that process, turkey after turkey after turkey, all night long. I estimate I personally caught sixty to eighty turkeys. There was a crescent moon in the dark sky, and electric lights strung to the shoulder-high fence around the turkeys. After about twelve hours of chasing and catching, we finished the job early the next morning. We rode back into town in the back of the same truck, with the low morning sun climbing up from the fields and lighting a gentle dawn. Then we all went out to a restaurant for a hearty breakfast of eggs, sausages, and big buttermilk pancakes soaked in strawberry syrup. It had been an exhilarating and surreal experience. I felt elated and also ready for college.

7

Deaf at a Hearing College

I SAT ACROSS A DESK from Morningside College's registrar, Mr. Ira Gwinn. In his late fifties, with black-rimmed glasses and dark eyes, he peered at me thoughtfully. "Mr. Hurwitz," he said, "you'll need to arrange support services to help you get through college."

I was offended.

"But I did fine in high school with no support services, sir," I pointed out.

"Still, you'll need them in college. College isn't high school," he said. "Here, you'll find that your professors rarely use textbooks for their classroom lectures, so you won't be able to catch what you missed by going to your books at night."

"I think I can give it a try without help," I said.

"No," he said firmly. "I'm afraid that having support services will be a condition of your enrollment. There's no point enrolling you just to set you up to fail. And don't worry, the Iowa Vocational Rehabilitation agency will cover the cost of a notetaker."

Having no choice, I relented.

Back then, "support services" didn't look like they do today. In 1961, no one had ever heard of a sign language interpreter, especially for college. Once in a blue moon, there would be a child of deaf adults (Coda) or a hearing person who learned how to sign from a church with deaf congregants, but that kind of interpreting was always done voluntarily. Since these "interpreters" didn't have any training, most of them would convey information consecutively, meaning they would listen to the speaker for a while and then ask the speaker to wait so they could summarize what was being said to the deaf person. Then they would watch the deaf person signing for a while, cut him off at some point, and summarize for the speaker what was signed. It was a very time-consuming process. Today, American Sign Language (ASL) interpreters are trained to facilitate communication simultaneously between both parties and are held to much higher standards professionally and ethically.

Having done very well in high school without the well-meaning intervention of hearing people demanding I use any particular remedy to even the playing field for myself in school, I wasn't looking forward to this sudden, late-in-the-game interference in my studies. All I could imagine it doing was slowing me down. I hadn't gone to CID for all those years, learned to speak and lipread, and mastered the challenges of attending a public high school to have my abilities completely discounted. But it seemed I had no choice but to go along with Morningside's plan for me. I grudgingly gave in.

Mr. Gwinn recommended that the college find a classmate who took the same courses I was taking. This hearing classmate could take class notes using carbon paper, and I would get the blue copy. We agreed that whoever was selected would have to be an outstanding student and be able to handle the rigors of not only his coursework but also of providing adequate notes for me. Mr. Gwinn thought that the classmate should also study with me and provide tutorial assistance as needed. It sounded like a feasible arrangement, but unfortunately, a few days after we'd drafted the plan, Mr. Gwinn called me back to his office to report that he was unable to find a classmate who met the expectations we had discussed.

"I did find one student, though, who might just do," Mr. Gwinn said. His name was Al, and he was from Chicago. Al took the same classes I was taking, but his high school grades weren't as good as mine. Still, Mr. Gwinn told me, Al was willing to be my notetaker, and he needed the money.

The next day in Mr. Gwinn's office, I met Al, a seemingly friendly guy with a chubby face and blond hair. He showed me a page from his notebook to check if I could read his handwriting, which seemed perfectly legible to me. We talked about our plans for a major—I was considering engineering and mathematics. Al was undecided, so he'd just signed up for the classes that seemed most interesting to him. We shook hands and agreed to see each other at our first class together, calculus, the next morning.

In class, Al and I sat next to each other, and I watched as he steadily took notes throughout the professor's lecture. The professor spoke quickly and paced back and forth at the front of the class, making it very hard to read his lips. What he was talking about, I wasn't sure. Most of the students in the class were taking notes, not just Al. I alone sat with my notebook open to a blank page. I might as well be back home at my parents' house, I thought, reading the textbook and trying to work out the material for myself.

I glanced back over at Al. I could make out a line he'd written in his notes from the professor's lecture: It was something about a Lagrange equation for rigid bodies in planar motion. Sounded very interesting. The classroom had a window, and I could tell by the way the trees were waving around that the wind was picking up.

After about three days of trying out the arrangement with Al, I told him that it wasn't working. His notes were good—I appreciated their thoroughness and the care he was taking to keep his handwriting neat—but basically, I was biding my time every day until the end of class when I could get my hands on his notes and find out what the heck the professor had said. I was bored and wanted to be a more active class participant than the arrangement made possible.

Al and I discussed several possible alternative strategies, and finally, I told him to forget about the carbon paper. Instead, I would sit next to him and copy his notes *as he was writing.*

"That way," I told him, "if I have a question in class, or want to say something to participate in the class discussion, you could say it for me, see?" The plan was that if I had anything to say or ask, I'd write it on a piece of paper and have him speak for me.

And it worked. Because I was reading Al's notes in real time, and his notes were such a good record of what was being said by the professor and even the other students, I was able to interject questions and comments, just by writing them quickly on my own notebook and gesturing to them, indicating to Al that this was to be shared aloud. Sitting shoulder to shoulder, focusing intently on the class together, Al and I came to understand how each other thought. To our amazement, we became close friends for the remainder of the academic year. We studied together, and I found myself tutoring him. Sometimes he had difficulty understanding a theory or how a formula is set up based on a mathematical word problem, and I'd explain how to solve these problems and answer his questions. And I'd ask him questions for clarification of his notes to better help us to understand the points made by the professor or the class discussion. By the end of the year, Al was a straight-A student.

As for me, I did okay grade-wise, but I didn't get straight As. I'm not sure why my grades were a little lower than Al's. Maybe it was because I missed the nuances of the lectures and discussions by being deaf. Maybe it was subjective because the professors didn't know me as well as they would have had I been able to participate in discussions on my own. In any case, we both benefited from our friendship and academic partnership.

MORNINGSIDE COLLEGE'S CAMPUS was tidy and attractive with brick and granite buildings, several newly built dorms, and a modern A-frame church. The campus also had large sycamore trees, a busy library, and a student union where we played cards at round tables and watched sports and news on the one large television pushed to the perimeter of the room, near tall windows. The students were mostly white, from Iowa, and male—the ratio of men to women was something around four to one—although there were a handful of people of color and international students as well. In fact, most of the students at Morningside were from right here in Sioux City and nearby northwest Iowa.

I'd grown up always aware of Morningside College's existence because it was one of Sioux City's three four-year colleges. I was a commuter student, and I returned home to my parents' house each night after classes and studying. (On my very first day of college, my mother announced that evening, "When you left this morning you were a boy, and you've returned as a man!")

I wasn't sure I was getting the full college experience, though, by still living in the same town, in my childhood house, with my parents. But it was a nice arrangement.

Over the Christmas break, I took a 560-mile train ride from Sioux City to St. Louis to see Vicki, who met me at the train station. Weeks earlier, to my surprise, Vicki's parents had invited me to stay as a guest at their house and had also kindly arranged for my visit to include meetings with some of my old teachers and friends from CID.

Vicki and I had been writing long letters to each other—fifteen-page, twenty-page, and even one thirty-seven-page letter from her to me— every week since the summer. In her letters, she shared news of friends we had in common, expressed frustration at her parents' strictness with her, wrote poems, and told funny stories. Through our letters, we learned about each other's backgrounds, lives, and hopes for the future.

VICKI WAS BORN in Richmond, Virginia, on February 6, 1944. Her mother, Irene Stutson Winer, graduated from Duke University and was a teacher who taught English, French, and piano. Vicki's biological father, Bernard Abraham Winer, who aspired to be a doctor, died when Vicki was two months old while serving as a reconnaissance photographer in the Army Air Corps during World War II. Irene and Vicki moved in with Irene's parents in Suffolk, a tiny town about one-and-a-half hours away from Richmond. Vicki's grandparents, with whom she was very close, hailed from Latvia and Lithuania; her grandfather owned a furniture business and was also into real estate.

Vicki's mother married Jack Bernstein shortly after they found out that Vicki was deaf when she was three-and-a-half years old. Jack, a New York City native, was a copy editor for the *Suffolk News-Herald*. Since her grandfather wanted an oral education for her, he went to the library to find information and identified three schools: the Lexington School in New York City, the Clarke School in Boston, and CID in St. Louis. Jack was a journalism graduate of the University of Missouri in Columbia but couldn't find a job in New York or Boston. The *St. Louis Post Dispatch* told him he needed a bit more experience in the newspaper field, so Vicki's family moved to Peoria, Illinois, where

Vicki as a toddler.

he found a job with the *Journal Star*. While on a waiting list to enter CID, she attended a self-contained classroom for deaf children at the Whitney Elementary School in Peoria for a year and a half.

Like me, Vicki had been a young residential student at CID—in her case, beginning when she was five-and-a-half years old when she started a one-year stay at the school until Jack finally got the position that he wanted in St. Louis. She then commuted to CID until she transferred to Dielmann Road Elementary School for the seventh grade. Every Monday while attending CID, she had a letter-writing assignment to her maternal grandparents and aunt in Suffolk, Virginia. For the eighth and ninth grades, she went to the brand-new Ladue Junior High School. During that time, she volunteered as a candy striper at the Jewish Hospital of St. Louis and was active with the B'nai B'rith Girls.

Vicki's mother constantly drilled her on her English skills, and her father encouraged her to read books. Since her father did a lot of free-lance work, she was encouraged to learn to type on her own from a library book. She often typed news releases from his written notes. She read every biography possible until he encouraged her to read other books too. She also wrote in her letters to me about her worries over schoolwork and tests. I encouraged her to do her best and to listen to her mother, who implored her to focus and excel. But Vicki didn't enjoy school much and thought she might want to be a professional dancer, rather than go to college but was told she didn't have much of a chance for a dance career because she was deaf. After graduating from Horton Watkins High School in Ladue, she decided to enroll at William Woods College (now University), a small women's college in Fulton, Missouri.

Like me, Vicki did not have any interpreting support in high school or WWC, but she stayed in touch with deaf people by volunteering at the nearby Missouri School for the Deaf. She enjoyed working with elementary school students and tutoring high school students. It was there that she began to learn sign language. Once she met my father, who communicated primarily through sign language, she was even more encouraged to learn how to sign and fingerspell.

Her letters were long and beautiful and fun to read. In mine to her, I told her about my friends and classes, my part-time job washing dishes at the Copper Kettle—a coffee shop by the bus depot—and my love of all things related to mathematics. We joked and traded random thoughts, endearments, and full accounts of our days.

In one letter, I wrote: "I showed Gary and Armella (his wife) the big picture of both of us. Armella admitted I am very lucky to have you. I told them that you might be coming for Thanksgiving, and I'd like for them to meet you. They'd love to meet you. Armella asked me if I missed you. I told her, 'Oh, yes, I miss her very much although it's been only three weeks since we saw each other. Besides, I got a thirty-seven-page letter from her yesterday.' Armella exclaimed, 'That's too much.' I talked back to her. 'Well, remember before you and Gary were married, you used to talk with Gary on the telephone for two to three hours, two or three times a day.' Gary said, 'Who me, I never did it' (slyly). I said, 'Oh baloney, every time I came over to see you, you were lying on the floor talking and talking and talking for hours and hours.' Armella then commented, 'Yes, that's true. And I don't blame you and your girlfriend for writing long letters.' HA!"

I'd made my point. For deaf sweethearts living in different cities, letters were the only available mode of communication. Every day, I made sure to make a stop at the mail room in the student union to see if there might be a letter for me from Vicki. Very often, there was.

Vicki and I on a date.

MY FIRST YEAR AT MORNINGSIDE was over, and the summer stretched before me. I would work, save money, and try to see Vicki in person again. My opportunity came in the shape of the National Congress for Jewish Deaf convention in Washington, DC. Vicki's family always spent summers in Suffolk and Virginia Beach, so while there, Vicki's parents drove to Washington so that she could attend the conference with me. I was going to it with my Uncle Max and Aunt Cranie.

On the first day of the convention, Vicki and I were in the hallway of the hotel, outside the small ballroom where the meeting was being held at the Washington Marriott Wardman Park hotel when my aunt and uncle stepped off an elevator and walked toward us. I couldn't wait for them to meet Vicki and for Vicki to meet them.

"Uncle Max! Aunt Cranie!" We greeted each other, and I introduced Vicki. How wonderful to have my favorite relatives meet my sweetheart, whose beauty and intelligence and friendliness were so apparent to everyone. One evening during the conference, I gave her my high school ring as a commitment, though I told her she was free to date others. She wore it on a chain around her neck. And the next time Uncle Max and Aunt Cranie visited our family in Sioux City, he took me aside in the kitchen and said, "Keep that Vicki!" Even though we lived more than ten hours apart by bus or car, and I was in college, and she was still in high school, I was going to try to do just that.

TO MY DISAPPOINTMENT, Al did not return to Morningside the following year because of financial difficulties. The news was like a dark cloud over me. I didn't bother seeking out a replacement notetaker through the registrar's office, knowing from experience how difficult it would be to find someone qualified enough, someone as good as Al. Instead, during the first few days of classes, I looked for a classmate in each class who took a lot of notes. I would sit next to him and explain that I was deaf and needed help with the notes. To my surprise and relief, each of the classmates I approached with this request was willing to share his notes with me, and also agreed to ask questions and make comments for me. Not only did this allow me to succeed in class, but it was also a fine way to develop some new friendships with my classmates. And as had happened with Al, many of my notetakers also became my study partners outside of class.

I had moved out of the house and into the dorms at Morningside. "I decided it was time for me to 'face the music,'" I wrote to Vicki about the move. My first roommate was an African American guy from Chicago who had played basketball at the legendary Loyola High School. He was one of only four or five Black students in the entire student body that year, and the first Black person I had ever spent more than five minutes with. We hit it off very well, but he left college after his first semester. My second roommate was Woody from Kansas City. When I went to Kansas City for Thanksgiving at my Aunt Sylvia's, he invited me to meet his family.

That year, I became very close friends with Cyrus Riahi, a classmate who hailed from Tehran, Iran. One time while hanging out in my room, he noticed and stared at a Star of David on my dresser. He asked if I was Jewish, and I said yes. He thought some more and said, "Oh well, it doesn't matter as long as we are friends." Cyrus was a charmer and dated a lot of women. He also gave me a gift—handmade silver, beautifully painted cuff links—to give to Vicki, even though they'd never met. Vicki proudly wore them with her blouses for years. After we graduated and even later in life, I looked for Cyrus high and low, but to no avail. I could never locate him. I often wonder how he is.

THAT SPRING ON CAMPUS, the cherry and magnolia trees were in full blossom, and their pink flowers littered the quads. The sidewalks, library, and student union were crowded with students. My classes were going well—they were rigorous and challenging—but I looked forward to transferring to Iowa State University in Ames, Iowa, for my upperclass studies. On the other hand, Ames was far away from Vicki too. Maybe I could find a way to get my education closer to her.

Vicki was a junior in high school, and we rarely saw each other, although we still wrote our long letters. What if we grew apart? What if she fell for a boy in her own city? I realized that if I wanted to do my best to ensure our relationship lasted, I should be closer to her. Greenville College, I discovered in my research, was located in Illinois about fifty miles east of St. Louis. Over spring break, I flew to St. Louis to visit with Vicki for a few days. While I was there, I would take a day trip to visit Greenville College.

THE BUS TO GREENVILLE left at six in the morning, and no bus returned from Greenville to St. Louis until late that evening, which would give me the whole day to explore the college and the town. I met with the admissions officers, who regaled me with the many special restrictions the college imposed on its students, especially third-year transfer students. For instance—and this was what bothered me the most—I'd have to park my car off-campus and leave the keys with the office because it was the college's policy for all students. On top of that, Greenville didn't even have an engineering program, which I should have checked about earlier.

I walked around the campus in a sullen mood. By 10 a.m., I was done. This was not the place for me. As much as I was eager to move on from Morningside and be close to Vicki, what would be the point of moving somewhere smaller, more restrictive, and less able to prepare me for my intended career?

My return bus wasn't due to depart until six that evening. I walked to the bus depot to see if other buses were going through other towns where I could transfer to another bus to St. Louis. There were none, so I decided to take a chance and hitchhike.

It was a hot day, and I was wearing a black suit and tie. The collar of my starched white shirt was scratchy and tight around my neck. I pulled on the back of it to make a gap and let in some air, but there was no breeze. The sun beat down, and sweat trickled down my back. Cars and trucks zipped by me without stopping, kicking up dust. Whenever I saw a car or a pack of cars nearing me, I stuck out my thumb and put a smile on my face; after two hours, I gave up. Nobody was in the mood to pick up a hitchhiker. I walked across the highway to hitch a ride back into Greenville. I'd have to pass the next five hours on a hard bench in the bus stop.

Then I saw an old car—rusty and blue and emitting black smoke from its tailpipe—chugging slowly over the hill heading west, on the side of the highway I'd just left. I ran back across both lanes and stuck out my thumb. To my great relief, the old car slowed and then stopped. "Come on, get in," the driver said.

At first, I was hesitant since he was unkempt and smoking a cigarette. His smile was friendly, though, and I really wanted to leave Greenville, so I opened the passenger-side door and lowered myself into the seat. He took off again, and the engine felt rough. I smelled burning oil. He asked me where I was heading, and I told him St. Louis. We talked a bit, and I found out he was from Ohio on his way to California.

"Look in the back!" he told me after a minute.

To my surprise, there on the backseat was an injured man stretched out, and his face grimaced in pain. The driver said he was looking for help for this man, that his back was broken. I wondered how he'd broken his back, but I decided against asking. Maybe he'd fallen, or been in a fight? But why wasn't he in the hospital?

"Now would be a good time," I thought to myself, "to get out of this car," but I watched the miles go by, hoping that we'd reach my destination without anything serious occurring. After about twenty miles, the driver said, "I'm getting sleepy. Can you drive?"

As I drove, I noticed that the gas gauge was nearly empty. "Should we stop for gas?" I asked. He said yes, and I stopped at the next gas station. As I pulled into the gas station lot, I noticed how tight the steering wheel was and that the brakes were nearly shot. It was all I could do to get the car to a complete stop at the tanks before running into them. He got out and filled up the car with gas, then leaned in the window and said, "Can you pay?" Fortunately, I had enough cash in my pant pocket and figured I should at least pay for my way since they were doing me a favor to let me ride. "Will you keep driving until St. Louis?" he asked me, and I agreed I would.

As we crossed the Mississippi River into downtown St. Louis, he told me to keep driving to my girlfriend's house. The request gave me a quick chill. I didn't want the injured fugitive or the car's owner to know, necessarily, where Vicki lived. At the very next red light, I shifted the car into park, got out, closed the door, and walked away from the car as fast as I could. Was he following me? I hazarded a glance back, but the car was still idling at the light, and the car's owner was still sitting in the passenger seat, his face expressionless.

I walked to the *St. Louis Post Dispatch* offices, where Vicki's father worked as an editor for the newspaper's TV magazine. As soon as I found him, I told him that my trip to Greenville hadn't worked out well and that I decided to come back early. I didn't tell him how I'd come back.

AT DINNER, we were five around the dining table—Vicki and I, her parents, and her adorable little sister, Jo Ellen, who was fourteen years younger than Vicki.

"Greenville College wasn't for me," I said, "so I'll keep looking around for something better."

"Why don't you look into Washington University, right here in St. Louis?" Vicki's mother asked me as she began to clear the dishes from the table.

Washington University? It was an elite school, one of the best private research universities in the country.

"I don't think I could get in there," I said.

"Well, it can't hurt to try!" Vicki's mother said, "Send in an application."

So, the next week, I did. Much to my surprise, I was accepted.

8

A Perfect Match

In the summer of 1963, I enrolled in two Washington University courses in a five-week summer session. My parents and I traded our cars so that I could drive their car, a 1956 Bel Air Chevrolet with its gold and yellow decor, to St. Louis.

After completing the summer coursework, which I'd found more challenging but also more interesting than anything I'd studied at Morningside, I flew to Sioux City to visit my parents and leave the car with Vicki. Upon return, Vicki and our friend Karen picked me up at the airport. I was shocked to see my beautiful car completely covered with grayish-white film.

"Karen and I thought we'd wax your car, as a surprise," Vicki confessed sheepishly.

They had applied wax but didn't buff it right away in the 95-degree weather. The wax had dried quickly. All of their diligent attempts to remove it had failed. I kept my cool, with great effort, smiled, and said I would take care of it. I bought a new can of wax, rewaxed small areas at a time, and immediately buffed. After four or five hours of work, the car ended up doubly shiny.

Washington University in St. Louis was impressively large and grand. While the sidewalks at Morningside had been cement, at Washington, the walkways were red brick. The buildings were imposing, built in a style called "Academic Gothic," characterized by towers and arches and columns. I could feel that it would be easy to go about your studies and be socially lost, never making meaningful connections. I thought it would be good for me to join a small group and perhaps get a head start on making new friends. I needed to join a fraternity, I decided.

I checked out three Jewish fraternities, my favorite of which was Zeta Beta Tau (ZBT) because the fraternity brother members were quite friendly and took the time to chat with me.

I also checked several other fraternities, including Sigma Chi, where many members were engineering students. On top of that, Sigma Chi had one deaf member already. He encouraged me to consider joining the fraternity, and although I liked ZBT, most of the members were premed, prelaw, or prebusiness; I had more in common with the Sigma Chi brothers.

After a few days of socializing with the Sigma Chi brothers, I had a feeling they would invite me to join their fraternity. On the last day of Rush Week, the president and vice president asked if they could have a private talk with me in one of the bedrooms at their fraternity house.

"We're very interested in you, Alan," the president said to me, "but we have one question." He hesitated, and my mind raced through what they might want to ask me. Was it going to be about deafness? After an awkwardly long pause, he asked, "What religion do you follow?" This had not been one of my guesses. I was taken aback.

"Is that important to you?" I asked them.

"Yes, it is," the president said.

I said, "Nice meeting you guys," and shook hands with them. I left the fraternity house, dazed and stunned. I walked around campus aimlessly for almost an hour, playing the scene in the fraternity house bedroom over in my mind. The looming buildings suddenly looked different, possibly sinister. What other pockets of bigotry were hiding here?

Walking toward me on the sidewalk was one of the ZBT brothers. He'd been looking for me, he said.

"We are waiting for you at the ZBT house. We want to invite you to join us," he told me with a smile. Surprised, I went over to the house and accepted their invitation right away. I felt comfortable with them; they were very friendly and accommodating of me as a deaf person. And I soon learned that there were indeed a few other engineering majors in the fraternity, which reassured me. Vicki and I loved to go to the fraternity parties together and enjoy music loud enough to make the floors shake, dancing, and drinking rum punch from a (new) garbage can.

Regardless of Sigma Chi fraternity's policy of religious discrimination, I interacted with some of their brothers in my engineering classes. We were friendly with each other and sometimes even studied together. Several months after the Sigma Chi brothers had asked me about my religion, the Washington University president publicly stated that any form of discrimination based on gender, race, ethnicity, or religion would be forbidden on campus, and this policy applied to all student organizations, including fraternities and sororities. Apparently, it was a prevalent issue with students, faculty, and staff on campus, and the president wanted to emphasize the policy with a public statement. I wondered what would have happened if he'd made this policy announcement before my arrival? As it turned out, joining ZBT was one of the most fortunate decisions I made in college.

In my first year at Washington University, I lived in a nice dormitory suite that had two bedrooms for two guys each, a single bedroom, a sizable bathroom, and a shared lounge. Michael Shamberg, who later became a movie producer (*The Big Chill*, *Erin Brockovich*, and many others) had the single room. Coincidentally, Michael went on to have a deaf son who attended NTID and Gallaudet University before graduating from the New York Academy of Art in New York City.

Michael and I were in the same ZBT pledge class as Harold Ramis, the actor, writer, and director who was in *Ghostbusters*, *Stripes*, and many other movies. Harold also cowrote *Animal House*, which my son believes was based on our fraternity experiences in the 1960s. It was in part but, according to Harold, it was also based on an amalgamation of hundreds of other true and apocryphal stories from many other fraternities and colleges around the country.

During Hell Week, our initiation period, our pledge class became a close and cohesive group of brothers. We had a lot of fun playing pranks on our older brothers in the ZBT house. Once, we told them about a "stag" party supposedly happening in another town about fifty miles away. Of course, when they got there, they quickly realized we had fooled them and returned to campus, fuming mad. By then, we had left for the University of Wisconsin in Madison for a weekend party with the ZBT brothers there, but not before locking some ducks in the house and "redecorating" the house with eggs. When we returned Sunday night, our brothers punished us by forcing us to cage the ducks, clean up the house, and observe and record duck behavior for several hours over two days.

During my first year at Washington, I enrolled in electrical engineering courses and continued to identify classmates who would let me copy their notes. Fortunately, many of my engineering professors were not native English speakers, so they wrote their own notes on the blackboard, section by section, from wall to wall, and back again to the first section, which they would then erase and begin again with the next section. Instead of copying notes from a classmate, I could copy them from the board and use my textbook to follow their lectures. I also took required courses in liberal arts—English, literature, history, economics, philosophy, math, and science—and copied notes from my classmates.

After the first semester, my department chair, Dr. Lloyd "Bob" Brown, called me into his office. He was concerned about my performance in the Introduction to Electronics course. He indicated that he realized I had a problem following his teaching in class. "But I think you could do better, Alan," he told me. He offered me two options: get a D in the course and move on to the next course in electronics or take an F and repeat the course. After we discussed the pros and cons, I ultimately decided to go with the F and repeat the course in the spring semester. As a result of my increased concentrated studying, I did very well and got an A. I also did well with the rest of my coursework in the electrical engineering program. I will never forget how kind, yet firm, Dr. Brown was with me, and I learned a great deal from him. Giving a student a second chance has stayed with me throughout my professional life, and I have come across many students who deserved and got a second chance from me, be it with their coursework or their behavior.

IN MY SECOND YEAR, Michael, Harold, and I moved to the ZBT fraternity house off campus, home to many parties and a launching pad to many university events. Vicki, who was in her last year of high school, attended parties at the house, where the brothers were always welcoming and friendly to her. Naturally, she made a great impression on everyone who met her because of her confident, warm, and bubbly personality. There was some recurring awkwardness, though, because every time I needed to make a date with Vicki, I had to ask one of the brothers to call Vicki's mother to make plans. I had no choice. Back then, there was no way for me to contact Vicki directly.

As I had at Morningside, I worked part-time at Washington University as a busboy in the dining hall. Two deaf female students attended Washington during my time, and both were friends of Vicki. The three of us often got together to chat as I wiped down tables and stacked clean plates and bowls into the dish caddies. Two other deaf students were commuters and took courses on a part-time basis while working full-time.

On Thanksgiving Day, we went to my grandparents' home so that I could introduce Vicki to them. We sat in their front room on the sofa, and my grandparents asked about Vicki's family, St. Louis, and her school. They knew Vicki and I had been dating for three years already.

"You must stay for dinner and eat!" my grandmother said as we were preparing to say our goodbyes. She grabbed my arm and looked up into my face imploringly.

I tried to explain that we couldn't stay long, as we needed to get back home for Thanksgiving dinner, but my grandmother was determined that we should stay, sit at her dining table, and eat all the food she put before us. So, we stayed and ate and ate.

When we finally got home to my parents' house, Vicki and I were so stuffed that I had to tell my mother that we couldn't eat anymore.

"What? You ate already? It's Thanksgiving!" She was furious, but she kept the dinner warm for us, and we ate it later that evening. I still chuckle every Thanksgiving when I think about my job chasing turkeys, although it clearly didn't change my Thanksgiving eating habits.

That holiday week, I took Vicki to all my favorite places in Sioux City, including my junior high and high schools, Grandview Park, my old newspaper route, and Coney Island Weiner for hot dogs. I told her that I normally ordered three hot dogs for myself and encouraged her to do the same. "No, way! I'll have just one," she said, and so I ordered four hot dogs. After Vicki finished her hot dog, she asked if she could have another one. When she finished her second hot dog, she asked if I could get her a third one. After that, each time we went to Coney Island Weiner, I'd order six hot dogs—three for Vicki and three for me!

Vicki and I traveled to Sioux City again in December 1964 to celebrate Chanukah with my family during my first-semester break from Washington University. On our first night there, I told her a white lie—that I didn't want to get engaged until long after I finished college and settled in a job. Vicki said, "Oh, okay." I could tell she was disappointed but scared to come on too strong by expressing her dismay. I felt half-bad for making her suffer, but the other part of me was gleeful at the prospect of surprising her. Would she be happy if I proposed very soon, just when she was getting used to the idea of waiting through many more years?

The morning after my white lie, I had a meeting with my Uncle Victor, the brother of my late Uncle Bill, who had given my parents a loan for my education at CID. I wanted to get Uncle Victor's advice on finding an engagement ring for Vicki. My parents knew my plans and were thrilled with what I was up to, and they kept it quiet so that Vicki wouldn't know. Uncle Victor took me to one of his friends who was a professional jeweler, and I was shown black velvet trays filled with diamond rings. I knew Vicki preferred an oval cut, but I was attracted to the marquise. I vacillated between the oval and the marquise, and the jeweler suggested that I take both of them and show Vicki the marquise first to see if she liked it.

With the rings in my pocket, I drove to the nearest Woolworths, a five-and-dime store, and bought a pink teddy bear. I threaded a ribbon through the marquise ring and around the teddy bear's neck and put it in a small paper bag. My plan was to walk up to her with the unremarkable paper bag, which looked like it might hold a sandwich or some baseball cards, and then pull out the pink teddy bear, which she would understand was a gift for her. Then she would see the beautiful diamond ring and know that I was asking her to be my wife.

I walked through the front door of my parents' house with the paper bag clutched in one hand, my heart beating hard in my chest. I looked around but didn't see Vicki. I had expected that she'd be at the dining room table or in the kitchen with my mother. I found my mother alone in the living room.

"Where's Vicki?" I asked.

"She's napping in your bedroom," my mother said, her eyes bright with excitement. She glanced down at the paper bag in my hand and smiled.

I went to my room, and there was Vicki, sleeping on her side, on top of the covers, her hands tucked under her cheek. I sat on the edge of the bed, waiting for her to wake up. She stirred, opened her eyes, and asked right away, "Did your meeting go well?"

"Yes," I said, handing her the plain paper bag. She sat up, opened it, and looked down into the bag. I pulled out the little pink teddy bear to give her.

"Cute!" she said with a little smile. "Thank you."

"Look again," I said. When her eyes landed on the ring hanging from the ribbon, she smiled uncertainly and looked up at me.

"Is it real?" she asked, to my dismay. Couldn't she see how the diamond sparkled?

I said, "Look again and more carefully."

Pulling the ring closer and turning it over in her fingers, she got a better look. Our eyes met again, and hers were full of such hope and love—a mirror of my own feelings.

"Really?" she said. "I thought you said we wouldn't get engaged until much later."

"Should I take it back?" I teased her, smiling.

"No, I love it!" We embraced and kissed. She slipped the ring off the teddy bear's neck and off of the ribbon and onto her shaking finger. She held out her hand and admired the ring.

"I know you wanted the oval cut," I said, "but I liked the marquise better. But would you like to see the oval cut?"

"No! I love it because you picked it out," she said.

Then she excitedly showed the ring to my mother, not knowing that my mother already knew. I felt that I had found and secured the most precious treasure for myself and that I had set the course for a happy life—not just for myself but for Vicki, my mother, and both our families. I glanced across the room and saw Vicki signing with my father, the person who had inspired her to learn to sign in the first place.

That evening, we had dinner at my grandparents' home with Uncle Victor and his wife Aunt Marcella. Uncle Victor offered to call Vicki's parents in St. Louis to tell them the good news. Her parents were thrilled. Her mother even advised us not to have a long engagement, so we agreed to marry after I graduated from Washington that following August. Based on Jewish tradition, Vicki's mother said our engagement should be no shorter than four months and no longer than eight months. August would be perfect. I asked Uncle Victor, who was nearing seventy, to be my best man at our wedding, and he gladly accepted. The next day, Vicki wrote a poem about our engagement:

December 28, 1964 (About 3 P.M.)

On Sunday, December twenty-seventh
You told me you made an appointment with
Your Uncle Victor to discuss college plans
And I did not ask you any questions.

On the December twenty-eighth morning
At the breakfast meal you were joking
And I did not know what you planned to do
But I asked you just what you were up to.

You answered with a "why?" and a "nothing."
So this queer thought of mine was subsiding
You left the table with a permissible excuse
And I continued to tell your mother the news.

You were gone for almost a second hour
And making me miss you all the more
I was sitting in your bedroom in Sioux City
When you returned home finally.

You had a paper bag in your hand
I first asked you how your appointment

With your uncle was and then
You answered with a simple "Oh fine."

A second later you took out of the bag
A small pink teddy bear stuffed and darling
And I said, "Oh Tracy, you did not
Have to do this," and from me, a kiss you got.

You told me to look at it again
I did, and I noticed on the ribbon
Around its neck, a beautiful ring was attached
"Tracy, is it real?" I asked.

So unexpected this surprise here
And I thought you bought it at the dime store
You told me to look at it again—I took the ring off the ribbon.

I then realized you were not playing a trick
So I gave you a kiss and a big hug
What a beautiful engagement ring you gave me
You had a wonderful taste in picking out a Marquise.

A few years later, she entered a contest during a Deaf community
event where she presented the poem in sign language to an audience
and won first prize. And, she still has the pink teddy bear today.

9

Early Marriage

No one would give me a job. At Washington University, we seniors were encouraged to start applying for jobs early in the fall semester, and many of my classmates were getting two, three, even four offers as early as November. Swirling around me were the giddy conversations about how tough it was to have to choose between several exciting and well-paid job offers. I had the feeling I was being left behind, and I wasn't sure why.

Determined to get a job (after all, I was going to be a married man in a few short months), I started visiting small engineering companies to inquire about openings in person.

"Your résumé is impressive," the man across the desk from me said slowly, his forehead creased in a frown. "But, you see, son, you have zero actual working experience as an engineer. I'm afraid we're really only interested in hiring engineers with some prior experience."

It wasn't the first time I'd heard this. It wasn't even the second time. No, I thought, of course I don't have previous experience as an engineer. I have been busy going to college!

Exasperated, I blurted out, "How in the hell am I supposed to *get* experience if everyone is requiring experience before they'll give me a chance to get experience?"

His smile was sympathetic. "It's true," he said. "Small companies can't afford to hire and train young engineers. That's why you should be looking at large companies, like McDonnell Company, which employs something like 45,000 people. That's the kind of place you should be applying to."

So, I applied to McDonnell and other large companies but got the same responses. Could my being deaf also be a factor in my not receiving any offers? I was beginning to think so. Maybe they didn't know how to work with a deaf employee. Maybe when choosing between deaf candidates and hearing ones, they'd always choose the hearing candidates.

One of the advantages of attending RIT/NTID or Gallaudet University is the support deaf and hard of hearing students receive with their job searches, be it a co-op opportunity, an internship, or a permanent job. Not only that, the students are provided with job search courses that cover résumé preparation, mock interviews, briefing and debriefing their co-op placements, and responding to questions related to employment practices. Gallaudet and NTID even offer workshops to area employers that teach employers about environmental/alert systems for employees with hearing loss, communication strategies between deaf employees and hearing coworkers, as well as assistive devices and access services that facilitate group communication in meetings and conferences. But in the 1960s, at Washington University, none of that was available.

May arrived and with it graduation. My friends and I walked across the stage and accepted our diplomas while our families watched from their seats in the bleachers. I was happy and proud, but also still in the limbo of the unemployed, plus I had two more classes to take over the summer.

Two weeks after graduation, I got a summer job as an architectural draftsman for a very small architecture company in St. Louis. Bill Blank, a deaf architect there, was instrumental in getting his boss to hire me. I hoped that working with the company for at least six weeks while I took my final two summer courses would give me the experience that I needed to get my first full-time professional job as an engineer. I assisted other architects on a huge project with the Holiday Inn headquarters by tracing the drawings from the preset designs for the architects to do their final production work. As I sat bent over the large drafting table drawing, I often thought of my Uncle Max. What a coincidence that here I was doing the same sort of drafting work that he had loved to do for forty years at Bailey Meters in Cleveland.

Our wedding was set for August 22. I hoped that I'd have a job offer before the big day. Sure enough, a telegram arrived for me on August 5: White Sands Army Materials was offering me a job as an electrical engineer, with an annual salary of $7,000 (about $57,000 in 2020 dollars) in New Mexico, over 1,000 miles away in the desert.

But when I told Vicki about the offer, she wasn't too happy. We decided to talk with her father and get his advice. I hadn't had any conversations with him about my job search so far. When he heard about all the places I'd visited, all the applications I'd submitted, he seemed surprised.

"Have you ever applied to McDonnell?" he asked me.

"Yes, I did," I told him.

"You know," he said, "I'd be happy to call my friend in human resources there."

I'd had no idea that he had a friend well-placed in McDonnell's HR office. He made the call the next day and told me to meet with his friend the following day in his office. I wore my best suit, brought my résumé with me, and explained to the guy that I had applied to Mc-Donnell several times but either got rejected or received no response at all. He was surprised, too, and looked for my application in his file cabinet. After not finding it, he went to another cabinet that was filled with inactive applications. That's where he found mine, marked up (with what words, I still don't know). He read my application and said, "Hey, you should have been invited for an interview!" He immediately called Dr. Dennis Joerger, the head of the plasma physics department of electrical engineers, who told me to come back the next morning for a meeting.

The next day, I suited up again and met with Dr. Joerger. We hit it off very well since he was easy to lipread and could understand me in a one-to-one situation. As both of us were trained electrical engineers, we had a fluent conversation in the technical jargon of our field. He spoke slowly and clearly. Sometimes he wrote down notes to be sure that we understood each other. We talked about his department's mission, which was to develop a ray-tracing system for the NASA Gemini project that would connect ground antennas with a radio system in a space capsule. He explained that as the space capsule reentered the atmosphere after orbiting the Earth, there would be a substantial heat crash that would burn the insulated cone cover of the space capsule and lose the radio connection.

"Let's take a little walk," he told me. "There are some people I want you to meet." He then introduced me to his team. At the end of our hour together, we shook hands by the elevator. "You'll hear from me soon," he said.

I left the McDonnell building exhilarated. For the first time in months, I felt optimistic about my engineering career and calmer about my impending marriage to Vicki.

That very afternoon, I received a call through Vicki's father from Dr. Joerger with an offer of $7,700 to be an associate electronics engineer. They wanted me to start working the following Monday.

"Could you ask him if I could start September 1 instead?" I asked my father-in-law, thinking of our honeymoon plans. Dr. Joerger said it was not a problem. Everything was right with the world.

Vicki and I got married on August 22, 1965, in the beautiful Temple Shaare Emeth in St. Louis, with its colorful, thirty-foot-tall stained glass Ark where the Torah scrolls were stored. Vicki's mother had wanted the wedding in a hotel, but Vicki really wanted to get married in a temple. After a much-heated discussion between mother and daughter, Vicki's father persuaded them to compromise by having the wedding in the temple and the reception at a hotel.

Coincidentally, our wedding day was also Uncle Max and Aunt Cranie's fifteenth wedding anniversary. They were thrilled when they learned of our wedding date and asked what we wanted for a wedding gift. Since they lived in Cleveland and knowing Uncle Max had a fear of flying, I told them to fly and attend the wedding as our gift. Though he was hesitant at first, they did it, and it broke the spell for them and airplanes. Afterward, they flew everywhere, even halfway across the Pacific Ocean to Hawaii!

The morning after our wedding, we left for our all-inclusive honeymoon package at French Lick Springs Hotel in Indiana, a sprawling golf resort in the Hoosier National Forest, situated at the foothills of a small mountain range. The waiter who was assigned to serve us at dinner that first night was gracious, fun, communicative, and accommodating. The food and service were perfect. The next morning we had the same waiter, but now, mysteriously, he was very cold toward us, walking by our table several times without serving us. We didn't understand why and kept trying to get his attention. When he finally served us, he was still cold and unfriendly. Vicki and I were puzzled.

Since the resort's package didn't include lunch, we drove around the town for a change of scenery and had a wonderful lunch at a café. As Vicki and I discussed the waiter's odd behavior, I suddenly realized that maybe he was upset that we hadn't left a tip for him, which we'd thought was included in the all-inclusive package. "We'll tip him double tonight," I said.

The waiter poured wine from a bottle into our glasses, his face sour. We thanked him nicely, and he nodded curtly, still unsmiling. When he brought our food, we smiled and thanked him, but still he was like stone. After dinner, I left enough money on the table to cover a tip for dinner the night before, breakfast that morning, dinner that night, and more. Maybe it would have a thawing effect. Sure enough, when we returned for breakfast the next morning, he beamed at us, truly happy to see his old friends—his charm from our first night completely restored. "That was it!" Vicki said as he walked away to put our order into the kitchen. It was a learning experience for two young honeymooners.

OUR LITTLE APARTMENT IN ST. LOUIS was on the second floor of a two-story building on Eager Street, near a bank branch, a gas station, and an A&P. It had one bedroom, a living room that included a small eating space, and a narrow kitchen with miniature appliances. In the back was a deck that held a lounge chair and a barbecue, and since we moved in at the end of the summer, this soon became a favorite spot to relax or entertain visitors. From the deck, there were steep stairs down to a postage stamp backyard where Vicki hung our clothes to dry after washing them at a laundromat two blocks away.

In the fall, Vicki transferred from William Woods College to Meramec Community College in Kirkwood, Missouri. After taking just a few courses, she decided it wasn't the right fit for her. She didn't enjoy going to school because she found it boring not to participate in

Wedding party with both families.

class discussions, and it was difficult to lipread teachers; again, interpreters were not available back then. Finally, she was driving to school on a snowy day when a car hit her from behind. She suffered whiplash and received medication and a supportive brace for her neck.

"I want to get a job," she told me one evening while she was still recuperating. She was fed up with school.

She worked as a bookkeeping machine operator at a bank and later at a shoe company before we decided to start a family. A year after we'd started trying, we finally got the good news: we were going to have a baby.

Vicki's OB-GYN, a man nearing retirement, was also her mother's doctor. He didn't offer much advice or conversation at her obstetrics checkups, which was frustrating because, like most first-time mothers, Vicki was bursting with excitement and questions. "He's taken good care of me for more than twenty years," Vicki's mother said.

Her due date was in early October, but in June, on Father's Day, Vicki went into early labor. She was only five-and-a-half months pregnant. We rushed her to the hospital, where she delivered our daughter, who weighed just one pound and five ounces. She was tiny but beloved, and she died thirty-six hours later. Vicki's mother's doctor, who had been away on vacation or for some other reason not on duty during the delivery itself, came into Vicki's room just once. "The placenta was not attached to the wall of the uterus properly," he told us, explaining why the baby had come early. "I'm very sorry," he said, obviously uncomfortable to be speaking with us as Vicki wept in her hospital bed.

Following the Jewish custom of using the first letter of a family member's name, we named our daughter Bonita Vera after Vicki's father Bernard and my Uncle Victor. We buried her in Norfolk, Virginia, where Vicki's maternal grandparents had an extra burial plot. Her death was a profoundly sad experience for us both, and it left Vicki wondering if she could ever risk another attempt.

10

Forks in the Road

"I HAVE AN ASSIGNMENT for you," Dr. Joerger told me in my first week on the job at McDonnell. He wanted me to develop a computer program involving complex mathematical formulas. The palms of my hands were suddenly sweaty.

"Programming is not my forte," I told him sheepishly. In fact, I'd flunked a brand-new elective course in introductory computer science at Washington University. I told him as much, and he shrugged and smiled, seemingly unconcerned.

"Don't worry about that," he told me. "Professors rarely knew how to teach computer programming, given that it's such a new field. Here," he said, handing me a stack of materials on FORTRAN that he'd lifted from the top of his filing cabinet.

I went back to my desk and started to study the scientific programming language right away, following the instructions in the tutorial materials, writing sample programs, and then testing the programs I'd developed. Within a few weeks, I was fluent.

Not only was I fluent, I was enjoying it. I loved programming so much that I taught other engineers how to write it, thinking they'd take to it as well as I had. Some liked it, but it turned out that most of the other engineers tended to shy away from it, preferring lab work in plasma physics.

Several weeks later, Dr. Joerger asked me if I thought about going to school for a graduate degree. No, I thought I was done with school forever. But he strongly encouraged me to continue with advanced studies, so I applied to Washington University. I wasn't accepted, which didn't surprise me, given the mediocre grades I'd earned patching together note-taking help and studying without the benefit of interpreting support.

In 1967, two years after I started at McDonnell Aircraft Corporation, the company announced a merger with Douglas Aircraft Company into a conglomerate called McDonnell Douglas Corporation. With Douglas's 60,000 employees and McDonnell's 45,000 employees, the corporation was faced with a critical need to pare down the number of employees. Dr. Joerger called me into his office.

"Alan, you have three options," he told me. "Move with the plasma physics department down to McDonnell's division in Orlando and continue your work as an electronics engineer with skills in computer programming. Your second option is to move to the McDonnell Automation Company in the next building and assume a new role as a senior numerical control programmer responsible for developing numerical control programs to operate large tool and die machines for making airplanes, jets, and space capsules. Your third option," he concluded, "is to leave the company."

"This is a tough decision," I said. "May I discuss this with Vicki and her family before giving you my answer?"

"OK, I'll give you three days. I'm sorry this is so sudden, but such is the nature of big mergers like this. Big changes are happening fast!"

That night at dinner, we discussed the three options. Neither one of us was keen about moving to Florida. We had too many ties in St. Louis, and I was still working on my master's degree, having started night school classes at St. Louis University two years earlier. We decided to go with the second option, staying in St. Louis. (Most of my colleagues moved to Florida, and I sometimes wonder where I would be today if I had gone with the team to Orlando, but I have no regrets.)

My new supervisor was Joe Sadonis, an older man and a true gentleman. My new job was to supervise and train two junior numerical control programmers as we wrote massive programs to automatically control large equipment that manufactured parts for airplanes and jets. Our programs incorporated all parameters, including tool selection, change of tools, feed rate, coolant, and cutting tasks. I wrote my FORTRAN instructions on programming sheets and submitted them to a team of keypunchers to punch the instructions onto IBM cards. Upon receiving the punched cards in long boxes, I'd review the printed copy for accuracy. Next, I'd make any needed corrections on them and return to the keypunchers for new punched cards. Each time I submitted jobs to keypunchers, the turnaround time was three days before I could take the next steps. In that case, I'd work on several projects simultaneously. Once the punched cards were fixed, I'd submit them to a team of computer operators for test runs on tape drives, which meant another day before I'd get the results and make additional corrections as needed. In those days, the mid-1960s, the computer room was made up of an IBM 360 mainframe with tape drives in an approximately 25-by-40-foot room. Today, our smartphones are far smaller yet more powerful than the old mainframe.

One day, as I carried a pile of three or four long rectangular boxes of punched cards for a single project, I stumbled, and they slipped out of my hands, the cards scattering everywhere on the floor. The programmers gave me "that's too bad" looks. Luckily, each punched card was numbered. On my hands and knees, I gathered the cards, putting them back in order, one by one.

THE YEAR 1968 was tumultuous—riots, assassinations, a war raging in Vietnam, wounded soldiers and body bags pouring back into the country, campus sit-ins, and takeovers. It felt like everything was being reassessed and challenged, including deaf people's education and career possibilities.

The biggest news in deaf education stemmed from a congressional act in 1965, signed by President Johnson, which provided for the creation of a national technical institute for deaf students, which would be hosted by an existing institution of higher learning. Many schools applied to be the host institution, but RIT in Rochester, New York, was selected as the winner. Not only was it a leading science and engineering school, but also it was coincidentally planning on relocating its campus from downtown Rochester to land on the city's outskirts, where it planned to erect many new buildings. This timing made RIT perfectly suited to offer a deaf institute prime real estate designed explicitly for deaf college students, rather than retrofitted to the purpose.

In 1968, NTID welcomed its first class of seventy students. The students took some classes only for deaf and hard of hearing students, but they also enrolled in RIT classes and could pursue RIT majors.

When I read about NTID, I was intrigued and thought back to when I was a youngster and wanted to be a teacher of deaf students. Maybe I could combine my engineering skills with my dream of becoming a teacher in a college environment. I requested an application for a teaching position, but to my disappointment, the response I got in the mail was an admission application packet meant for a student. Rather than write to them again, I decided to let it go and continue with my graduate studies. Later, I would look back on that decision as fated.

Soon after sending away for information about NTID, Vicki was pregnant again, and we steeled ourselves for the journey, our past tragedy still fresh and painful. That fall, Vicki got very sick with H3N2, a flu virus that caused a pandemic between 1968 and 1969. H3N2 would go on to kill a million people worldwide, about 100,000 of them in the United States. Her new obstetrician, Dr. Ira Gall, was confident she would pull through, and the unborn baby would be just fine. When the five-and-a-half-month mark passed, and then the sixth and seventh and eighth months, we breathed easier and easier.

Bernard was born nine days past his due date, in late spring of 1969, big and healthy. The doctor had been right. Since we wanted to use Vicki's father's name, Bernard, our son was named Bernard Reuben after my Uncle Bill Mazie and my grandmother Rose Hurwitz. A few days after Vicki and Bernard arrived home, we had the bris ceremony at home, and the baby received his Hebrew name, Baruch Reuven.

One day, while Vicki was changing Bernard's diapers, he spoke his first word: "Block!" He was turning a blue wooden block over in his chubby baby hands as she pinned his diaper closed, and they were looking at each other when he said it.

"Yes!" Vicki signed and spoke back to him, delighted, "block!"

We didn't know if our son was deaf or hard of hearing or not, but we knew that no matter what, early language development was important, and so we had exposed him from his earliest days to language all the time. We talked to him and read books to him. He enjoyed listening to us while we pointed at the words and pictures. Books were part of our daily lives.

When Bernard was six months old, we took him to CID for his first hearing test because of the genetic history in my family. Although we were told that Bernard had no detectable hearing loss, the audiologist, Dr. Irvin Shore, explained it was too early to be certain. He advised us to bring Bernard back in six months. But when Bernard was a year old, we didn't take him back for his hearing test because he was talking and very responsive to everything around him.

One day around that time, Vicki said to her mother, "I was vacuuming under the crib yesterday, and Bernard didn't wake up." Her mother, who had never fully come to terms with Vicki being deaf, didn't like this tidbit at all.

11

A Lifetime Commitment

"READ THIS!" Vicki said, handing me a long roll of TTY conversations from the day. I took the paper and pulled her in for a kiss before placing them and my briefcase on the table. "Let me get my coat off first!" I teased her. Our little kitchen was filled with warmth and the delicious smell of homemade pasta sauce made with basil and oregano from Vicki's windowsill herb garden. It was almost 9:00 at night, and I was tired from working at McDonnell and then attending night classes at St. Louis University, but reading the conversations between Sally and Vicki was always one of the highlights of my day. I hung up my coat while Vicki served the pasta into two big bowls. Bernard, who had dinner hours ago, was in his crib in our room, asleep. I sat and read the day's exchange with Sally. Here were intimate details and thoughts about their lives as mothers of small kids, their families and friends, and current events. When I got to something especially interesting, I stopped to ask Vicki questions. Their conversations let me be in touch with her thoughts and feelings, and I felt lucky. How many spouses had a chance to read, verbatim, everything their spouse had said to a best friend earlier in the day?

Vicki and I had many friends in St. Louis, and I was active in several different organizations. I played softball with members of the Bell Club. I also was a member of the St. Louis Chapter of the Missouri Association of the Deaf and Central Institute for the Deaf Alumni Association (CIDAA). I was continuously interested in focusing on civic and advocacy activities because I was concerned about the civil rights and quality of life of deaf and hard of hearing people. I felt strongly that I was lucky—with my college degree (a rarity among deaf people then) and my supportive family and in-laws, with my wonderful wife and network of friends. So many other deaf people were being left behind because of a system and society that seemed stacked against us.

My first stab at community advocacy and a leadership role was with CIDAA. I was impressed with the alumni association's many outstanding leaders who displayed skills in running meetings using parliamentary procedures. At our reunion in 1966, I ran for president of CIDAA and was surprised to be elected even though there were older and more experienced candidates. Paul Taylor, who was Vicki's friend Sally's husband, was elected vice president, Vicki was elected secretary, Bill Sheldon treasurer, and Sally Taylor as the newsletter editor.

IN MAY 1970, I received my master's degree in electrical engineering. I was fortunate that McDonnell Douglas Corporation had a very generous tuition reimbursement plan. It required employees to first pay for a course, and if we got a B or better, we'd be reimbursed for half of the tuition. After I completed my master's program, I got a check for half of my cumulative tuition! Vicki and I used the money to purchase a brand-new royal blue four-door 1970 Chevrolet Impala.

Around that time, our friend Paul was invited to Rochester for a job interview at NTID as an assistant educational specialist for deaf majors in the College of Engineering at RIT. Paul had graduated from Georgia Tech with a bachelor's degree in chemical engineering and received his master's degree in operations research from Washington University in St. Louis. He was a chemical engineer at Monsanto Chemical Company after a stint at McDonnell as an operations research engineer. After the interview at NTID, Paul got the job offer but turned it down since Sally was pregnant with their third child and didn't want to relocate.

"Paul recommended me for that job he was offered at NTID," I told Vicki at dinner. Paul had told Dr. Victor Galloway, the director of technical studies at NTID, that he should invite me to apply.

Our first TTY.

A week later, I received a letter inviting me to Rochester for an interview with one of the NTID faculty members, my old friend Lyle Mortenson, who was the educational specialist for deaf students in the College of Engineering at RIT. During our earlier days as softball players in the Midwest Athletic Association of the Deaf tournaments, Lyle and I got to know each other pretty well, and I liked the idea of possibly working with him.

First, I wanted to see what Dr. S. Richard Silverman, the director of CID, had to say about the opportunity. Maybe he'd have advice for me before my interview. "It's a great opportunity!" he told me. He excitedly opened a drawer in his file cabinet, which was filled with his work as the chairperson of the National Advisory Committee on Education of the Deaf. This committee had been responsible for designating RIT as the host university for the establishment of NTID. "By all means, go for the interview! I think you'll be a good fit for NTID," he told me.

"Maybe I'll work at NTID for three years and then come back to St. Louis," I said, explaining how the thought of leaving a city where we had such deep ties was unsettling.

"No, Alan," he said to me. "This should be a lifetime commitment if you get and take this job offer. It would be choosing a path, a good one, but there's no turning back."

On May 5, 1970, the day before I was to fly to Rochester for the interview, I was scheduled to take my oral exams as a final requirement for my master's degree. Upon arrival at the St. Louis University campus, I was surprised and puzzled to see many students walking around with posters protesting the bombing of Cambodia by US military forces. There were no captions on TV, so I had no idea what was going on. When I learned that there had been a shooting massacre by the members of the Ohio National Guard at Kent State University the day before, I wasn't sure if my oral exams would commence. With my briefcase, I was able to enter the building after walking through a cluster of protesters. I was relieved to see the committee of faculty members and the department chair waiting for me in a second-floor classroom. I went ahead with my oral exams—remember, there still were no interpreters in those days, and so we used the blackboard to communicate with each other. I wrote down most of my responses on the blackboard and continued to converse with the committee to be sure that everyone understood my responses. I was not comfortable speaking in front of a group. After I was told I passed the exams with flying colors, I breathed a sigh of relief and headed straight to the airport for Rochester.

As our airplane descended from the clouds, I saw that Rochester was covered in snow. It was May. Inside the terminal, I expected to be greeted by Lyle, whose name was listed next to "Rochester airport" on the itinerary they'd sent me. I looked around at the rushing businesspeople, the families pulling bulging suitcases, the student types with backpacks slung over their shoulders. I couldn't find Lyle. Outside, I gaped at the amount of snow on the ground and took a cab to my hotel.

After a good night's sleep, I awoke early to be ready for breakfast with Lyle. Still, he didn't show, so I ate breakfast alone and took a cab to RIT. It was a huge campus with about 1,400 acres and brand-new brick buildings—giant brick dormitories, some eight stories high, on one side of the school, and on the other were the academic and administrative buildings. Connecting the two sides was a long, straight walkway called the Quarter Mile. It was a very new campus, only occupied by RIT since 1966, when the university had moved from its downtown location where it had been since 1829. As I walked around, a cold wind blew, bending sparsely planted young trees.

I found my way to Dr. Victor "Vic" Galloway's office at the College of Engineering in Building 9.

"Lyle didn't show up," I mentioned to Vic. "I hope he's OK."

Instead of responding to my concern, Vic encouraged me to proceed with the interviews for the day. He also informed me that due to the Kent State shooting two days earlier, both NTID Director D. Robert Frisina and NTID Dean William E. Castle had to reschedule and go to the congressional hearings in Washington, DC, that day.

"Oh, excuse me," he said when he received a video call from John Kubis, NTID mathematics department chair, on a Vistaphone.

"Is that a video call?" I asked, fascinated. I had never seen one before.

"Stay, join us in the conversation!" Vic said. It was an eye-opening experience. When he hung up, he said, "There are seven Vistaphone units on campus." Their placement on the 1,400-acre campus was limited, he explained, by the forty-foot-long cables that connected the units. It was not until thirty years later in the 2000s that we finally had videophones for video-relay services and point-to-point video calls. Nowadays, of course, we can easily use video on our smartphones as well.

At the end of a day full of interviews with various people and groups, I was back in Vic's office for a wrap-up.

"Although you're being interviewed for the *assistant* educational specialist position, Alan," he said, "I believe you have the qualifications and talents to fill in as an educational specialist."

I wondered, again, what might have happened to Lyle, who was supposed to hold that role already. I learned later that he indeed had left RIT for personal reasons.

As I was getting ready to leave for the airport, Vic asked if I could stay for a few more hours since Dr. Castle had just returned from

Washington, DC, and wanted to meet with me. Although I knew I needed to get to the airport to catch my flight back home, I agreed. After having a very lively chat with Dr. Castle, I rushed to the airport with no time to spare.

About a week later, I received a letter from Dr. Castle. It was a job offer. I would be a faculty member responsible for serving as an educational specialist for engineering students with an annual salary of $13,000, the same as my salary at McDonnell Douglas. Vicki and I were excited at first, but soon Vicki got cold feet. "No," she said, "I don't think I want to move." But then a few days and some weeks later, she said, "Okay, let's go," but by then, I'd changed my mind and didn't want to go. We went back and forth like that for the next three months. Even though this was a once-in-a-lifetime opportunity, we were so settled in St. Louis, and Bernard was just a year old. And on top of that, Vicki's mother was very upset with the idea that we might be moving away.

In late June, I attended the A. G. Bell convention in Philadelphia to interact with deaf and hard of hearing adults interested in meeting with parents and teachers of young deaf children. When I ran into Bill Castle and his wife Diane, he unsurprisingly asked if I would accept the job offer or not.

"Could we meet in private to discuss it?" I asked him.

"Sure. Let's go up to my room," he said.

Once we had the privacy of a room, I said, "I am very excited about the opportunity, and I'm grateful for the offer, but I want to make sure my wife Vicki and I are of one mind about this before I accept." I also told him that the salary they'd offered was not an increase from what I was making at McConnell Douglas.

"We'll pay you $14,000, then," he said immediately. I felt that the pressure to accept had just doubled.

"Let me talk to Vicki one more time. I promise I'll get back to you as soon as I've talked with her."

"OK," he said, "please do."

At home, I shared the good news with Vicki about an increase in the salary, and we both decided that I should accept the job. But I was worried that we would continue to have a problem with her mother, who was very upset about the whole thing. I got in touch with Vicki's

William "Bill" Castle.

father and asked him to meet me for lunch near his office. We had a great talk, and I mentioned my hesitancy about accepting the offer. Jack asked me why I was concerned, and I told him I was worried about Irene's reaction to the idea of us moving away. He told me to move on and accept the job, as he believed it was a great opportunity that would open doors to my future.

"You kids should not let Irene's feelings stop you. Let me take care of Irene."

That settled it, and in late July, I told Dr. Castle that I would accept the job offer starting on September 1, 1970.

12

"Get Busy!"

KNOWING THE ROOM number, I went in search of my office on my first day at my new job at NTID. Here it was, a small utility room on the first floor of Building 9. Dr. Astor, a hearing faculty member who was one of two assistant educational specialists, was already there, sitting at one of three desks, along with our secretary, Louise Chatfield, a grandmotherly person who really took care of all of us, including all of the program's students. We were to share the space. The third assistant educational specialist, located in another office, was Warren Goldmann, a young deaf faculty member and graduate of Stanford University with a bachelor's degree in electrical engineering.

At my first meeting on my first day, my direct supervisor, Dr. Victor Galloway, announced he would be leaving for a job at the Model Secondary School for the Deaf (MSSD), a high school for deaf and hard of hearing students at Gallaudet College (now University), in three weeks. I was surprised and disappointed at the news because I had been looking forward to working with him.

"Stay at my house until you find a place," Warren told me that first week. He was one of the first three people in Rochester to have a TTY at home, so I used it to contact Vicki in St. Louis in the evenings after work.

About three weeks later, Vicki flew to Rochester to spend a few days with me and look at houses. Our home in St. Louis was a ranch-style house with three bedrooms and two baths, and we wanted something similar or better here. Unfortunately, most houses in Rochester were two-story colonials that had one-and-a-half baths. We found a house we liked very much in the Village Green subdivision in Penfield off Whalen and Baird Roads, but felt that it was too far from RIT, so we didn't make an offer. We agreed it would be best if we could find an apartment to live in while we took a year to find a house to our liking. We found a nice place at Crittenden Way Apartments, a stone's throw from RIT, with stores and restaurants nearby. My drive home for lunch every day was without traffic, over winding, back roads along the Genesee River. It was on my drives that I gauged and appreciated the seasons, driving through rain, sunshine, snow, blooming trees and flowers, and bright fall foliage and falling leaves. Like St. Louis, Rochester was a real city, with cinemas and great restaurants and sports teams and leagues and conference centers and clubs, but also like St. Louis, it had beautiful rural spots immediately outside of the city center.

Soon after Vicki flew back home, our house in St. Louis sold, thanks to her father's real estate knowledge. After we arranged to close the deal, we packed up our things for the move. Vicki, Bernard, and I were finally together in mid-October after I flew to St. Louis and drove our car to Rochester.

At last, my family was with me! At lunchtime nearly every day, I drove home so we could eat lunch together in our kitchen. And when I was back at the office, Vicki enjoyed walking with Bernard in his stroller over a tiny wooden bridge across a creek, taking him to the stores each day since our refrigerator was rather small.

I went to my first college-wide meeting with NTID Director Dr. Frisina, who led a discussion with faculty and staff. Engrossed by the new experience of having a professional interpreter, Mickey Jones, at the meeting, I marveled at being able to understand everything. Wow! I was enthralled with this new experience and had goosebumps throughout the session and afterward. I had never before had full access to communication in large groups or professional settings. This experience made me realize how much I had missed not only in group meetings but also in the classes I'd attended in college. I felt this was a new beginning for me.

There were twenty-plus deaf students in various engineering programs in two different colleges at RIT. Our role was to support and provide them with tutorial assistance and make arrangements for interpreting and note-taking services in each student's class. Here I was, helping students the way I wish I had been helped during my own college career.

Later, as our responsibilities increased, I hired Dominic Bozzelli, who was hearing, as the third faculty member on the support team. He was a Notre Dame graduate with a degree in mechanical engineering. As we expanded to include a newly formed computer science program, I hired another hearing man, Jim Chmura, as a fourth faculty member. Stemming from this was an amazing team forming the ICCE (Institute College and College of Engineering) support department, and I became a department chair. We had fun working closely with students and faculty in the ICCE, comprising engineering technology and computer science programs. When my schedule allowed, I taught courses in math, physics, electronics, and computer science.

In the next four years, I had different supervisors—Dr. Castle, Dr. Jim Speegle, Dr. Robert Gates, Dr. Jim Collins, and Dr. Milo Bishop—all hearing. During that time, the ICCE team and I moved to four offices in the building while we expanded for faculty offices, a tutorial room, a study room, and a lab for our students.

I thought about applying to the Leadership Training Program (LTP) at California State University at Northridge (CSUN) since, at that time, it was a hot spot for those who wanted to get a master's degree in administration and supervision. I asked Dr. Frisina to get his insights on whether I should pursue a second master's degree. His answer surprised me. He discouraged me from attending the LTP; he suggested instead that I could develop my management and leadership skills *on the job*. "There are so many good role models and mentors right here on campus who could guide you on your professional development," he said. "I for one would advise you to get a PhD," he said. I thanked him for his advice, but I didn't have the motivation to pursue my doctorate at the time, so I put the idea in the back of my head.

Sometime later in the following year, Dr. Mac Norwood, a charming deaf man full of energy and intelligence who was known as "the father of closed captioning," came to NTID for a meeting. At the time, he served as the branch chief of educational technology at the US Department of Health, Education, and Welfare. We knew of each other but had never met, so he came into my office to chat. His smile was impish and his signing quick.

"You need to think seriously about going for a doctoral degree!" he told me. I shrugged. "Not sure how that would benefit me," I said.

He stood up and said, "Alan, get busy! When I got an honorary degree from Gallaudet College, I felt bad that I hadn't really earned it. It wasn't a real doctoral degree, you see?" He went on to tell me that this feeling of dissatisfaction propelled him to the University of Maryland, where he completed all requirements for a doctorate.

"We need more qualified deaf people to earn doctoral degrees because it will level the playing field for the deaf leaders of tomorrow! Think about it!"

After he left, my office felt strangely still and small.

I solicited insights from my supervisor, Dr. Bishop. Like Dr. Norwood and Dr. Frisina, he strongly encouraged me to pursue doctoral studies. "But why?" I asked him. "I'm interested in knowing what data you are relying on to make this suggestion."

"Because I have high hopes for your progressive leadership development. You could go far. But you currently have two marks against you, career-wise," he said. "You're deaf, and you only have a master's degree. You can't change being deaf. Go for your doctorate. I know it will open doors for you in the future."

Now three men I respected had urged me to pursue a doctorate.

In late 1974, there was a big leadership shuffle. Dr. Castle became the NTID director. Our former director, Dr. Frisina, was promoted to the senior vice president for institutional advancement for RIT. Dr. Bishop was appointed as the dean of NTID, and he asked me to be the director for the Office of Support Services and take over the Office of Interpreting Services and training programs for interpreters, notetakers, and tutors.

I was reluctant to leave the ICCE team because I enjoyed working with the students and the team. Dr. Bishop explained that he needed me to manage and train support services personnel and that I was ready to move on and assume more significant responsibilities. Jim Stangarone, the original coordinator for interpreting services, had just stepped down to take on new responsibilities in the admissions office. I agreed to take over, despite not wanting to leave the ICCE team and students. Luckily, the change of duties still allowed me to continue with teaching as a part of my overall faculty responsibilities. I moved to an office in a dorm room on the opposite side of the RIT campus, on the second floor of Ellingson Hall in the new NTID complex, which included the LBJ building, the Peterson and Bell dormitories, and the Shumway Dining Hall.

Now I had a team of five full-time and seven part-time interpreters, forty student interpreters, a scheduler, and a secretary. Lavina Hept, a scheduler under Jim Stangarone's stewardship, continued to work with me. Bless her heart and soul—with her institutional memory of interpreting services, she helped me get started quickly. I hired many new interpreters, both experienced and newly trained. I continued to increase the number of full-time interpreters to meet student demand over time. I also initiated a strategy to improve the compensation plan for interpreters. I was concerned about recruiting and retaining highly skilled interpreters, and I believed better pay and enhanced working conditions were the best way to attract them to NTID. It was critical to ensure that NTID was viewed as a competitive market for highly skilled interpreters, so that our students would benefit from having the best interpreters in their classes, giving them real access to the material and classroom activity. Today, RIT/NTID has 150 full-time professional interpreters, over 200 student notetakers, and fifty real-time captioners, likely the largest cadre of access service providers at any university in the world.

13

Bernard and Stefi

"BERNARD'S TEACHER is worried that he is so quiet," Vicki reported to me one evening.

"He's shy," I said. "But he talks plenty here at home."

"I know," Vicki said, frowning. "Let's record him talking and singing and give Mrs. Barbara Kutner, the nursery school teacher, the tapes," she said. It was a good idea. We started that evening, recording him during dinner. Afterward, we rerecorded him as he sat on the family room rug playing with his toy trucks, talking and singing songs.

The next day, we shared what we'd recorded with Mrs. Kutner, who was surprised to hear Bernard's voice on the tape.

"I think you should get his hearing tested nonetheless," she told us. Vicki was offended. Was the teacher suspecting Bernard of hearing problems just because we were deaf and despite the evidence on the tape? "Given our family history of deafness," I said, "I have to agree. Let's get the test done again. It can't hurt."

This time, the results showed that Bernard had a significant hearing loss somewhere between moderate and severe, beginning with about a 55-decibel loss at the beginning of the speech range, a curve downward across the speech range, and upward after the speech range. This meant that he could probably hear deep voices, usually men, within two or three feet.

"But by all means," the NTID audiologist said, "see another audiologist and compare the results." We took his advice and made a second appointment, this time with an audiologist in an ear, nose, and throat practice.

In the waiting room, Bernard sat on Vicki's lap as I leafed through an issue of *Life* magazine from the coffee table in front of me. The audiologist came, gave us a perfunctory greeting, took little Bernard's hand, and walked away with him, out of the room and down the hall. I leaped to my feet and quickly jogged after them. "Please wait," I said, "until after we've chatted first!"

"We'll chat when the test is done," he said.

"Well, I will come with you to the testing room then," I said.

"No, you stay in the waiting room," he said and then turned and walked away, dragging Bernard with him by the arm. Bernard looked back at me, obviously frightened. By now, Vicki was with me in the hallway. We both stood there, stunned. Should we chase the audiologist and wrestle with him for our boy?

A few minutes later, the audiologist returned with Bernard. "He's uncooperative. I can't test an uncooperative child."

"Repeat the test, but with us in the room!" I said.

"That's not how we do it in this office," he said.

"I insist!" I said, and the audiologist had to relent.

Bernard sat on Vicki's lap while I watched. The audiologist was clearly rude and uncommunicative. He insisted that Bernard, wearing headsets, respond to him when he heard sounds. At first, the audiologist handed Bernard an abacus with colored beads for him to move from one side to the other each time he heard a sound. Bernard was unresponsive and uncooperative. It was clear that our son was frightened and didn't know what was expected of him. As tactfully as possible, I told the audiologist that it was not working at all and asked if I could help out. He waved his hand as if to say, "Fine!"

I put a handful of pennies in my hand and told Bernard, "Let's play a game. When you hear a sound, you let me know, and I'll give you a penny." Bernard was suddenly cooperative, and he collected a lot of pennies. I could tell that the audiologist was amazed, but of course, did not admit it.

"I'll share the test results with the doctor, who will, in turn, share them with you." He left us, and we were relieved to be done with him.

Vicki, Bernard, and I went into the doctor's office and waited for what seemed like forever. Finally, he ducked in to speak with us, but almost immediately his secretary called him out to see a sales clerk, leaving us again alone, waiting and wondering. After a while, the doctor came back as if in a rush. "I'm sorry, folks; I have lunch to go to with one of my associates."

I said, "Hey, wait a minute. We must talk with you." He grudgingly sat down and wrote a note saying that Bernard had "inner ear deafness," which we didn't understand.

"What is 'inner ear' deafness?" I asked. He said nothing, but stood and glanced at the door. "Folks, I really have to go. You should make an appointment with another audiologist, at the hearing and speech clinic." Then he was gone.

Astounded, Vicki and I walked out with Bernard. We hadn't been treated with such disrespect in a long time.

Vicki and I looked at each other and asked, "So that is what hearing parents experience when discovering their child is deaf?" Many young parents back then, and even today, have received such biased information from audiologists or do not receive appropriate support from them. We later met with an audiologist, Mrs. Kendra Marasco, at the Al Sigl Hearing and Speech Center. She was very warm and friendly, and we loved her. She determined that Bernard would benefit from a hearing aid and that he would need a regular twelve-week training on how to use his hearing aid and to work on some parts of his speech. In each session, Vicki observed the training through a one-way window. A three-and-a-half-year-old hard of hearing boy was also in the "class." After five weeks, Mrs. Marasco told us there was no need to continue with the training since Bernard was doing very well. She also mentioned that she was impressed with his language development, which, at that time, was equivalent to that of a six-year-old. Clearly, Bernard was exposed to both spoken and sign languages, while the other boy's hearing parents used only spoken language and didn't know sign language.

Bernard was fitted with hearing aids and continued to attend the nursery school. At the same time, because Vicki's mom had enrolled in the John Tracy Clinic Correspondence Course for new parents with young deaf children and had found it helpful, Vicki signed up to use the course with Bernard. John Tracy was the deaf child of the legendary actor Spencer Tracy and his wife, Louise Tracy. They founded the correspondence program after realizing how many other young parents were struggling to know how to raise and educate their deaf children.

The following year, we enrolled him in the privately run two-room Farm School that had very small classes. He was not happy and was uncommunicative and uncooperative with the teachers. Every morning, we had to drive him to school because he refused to get on the school van. It got to be so bad that the teacher suggested Bernard see a child psychologist. Naturally, we were affronted but decided to find one. After a few private sessions with an excellent child psychologist, we were told to let Bernard attend a public school. "He's advanced academically," the psychologist told us.

"But how will he fare socially in a big public school?" we wondered. Just the thought of him being ostracized and confused in a large school filled us with panic. "He's so shy!" we said. But the psychologist suggested Bernard's social skills would come with ease as he developed his academic skills in a school better matched to his great potential. As we discovered later on, the psychologist was right.

Bernard began first grade at Baird Road Elementary School near our home. Its truly wonderful principal Mr. Ted O'Brien took Bernard under his wing; Bernard benefited from his nurturing guidance. Having been trained as a counselor, Mr. O'Brien succeeded in encouraging Bernard to become comfortable with interacting with his classmates and teachers.

Another stroke of luck took place when Mr. O'Brien received a grant to establish a new program, Project Challenge, for gifted children. Bernard was selected to participate in the project with his three best friends from our neighborhood. While the other students worked in regular classrooms, he and his friends were pulled out periodically to participate in more complex and challenging assignments, such as doing research and going to the library. The selected students were called "the challengees" and the teachers "the challengers." The project continued throughout Bernard's elementary years.

By 1974, when Bernard was five years old, Vicki had had three more failed pregnancies. Each pregnancy had come with joy, trepidation, fervent hoping and praying, and then crushing disappointment. Neither of us wanted Bernard to be an only child. Not only did we know he'd be a wonderful, caring older brother, but we wanted him to have the benefit of having a sibling. Even though I'd been an only child myself, growing up in residence at CID had made me feel I had many brothers, and Vicki had two younger sisters.

Our Rochester friends Bill and Mary Ann Darnell and Harry and Pat Scofield had adopted their children with much success, so we felt this was our answer. We would adopt.

The Monroe County Social Services housed a public adoption agency. Within the first few months of working with the agency, Vicki got pregnant for the fifth time. We decided that, if it were a girl, we would name her Stephanie, after Vicki's maternal grandmother, Sadie Stutson. The agency told us the adoption process couldn't be continued until after the baby was born. Vicki, who had a premonition her pregnancy wouldn't be successful, asked the caseworker, "What if I lose this one?" The caseworker, somewhat flippantly and coldly we thought, said simply, "Well, if you lose it, come back." We decided not to go back there ever again.

Vicki's premonition proved correct, and her pregnancy ended in a miscarriage. Not wanting to return to that public agency, we checked with an attorney we knew, Joseph Kaufman, for a recommendation. He suggested a private adoption agency, Northhaven, next to Rochester General Hospital (Northside). Anne Lane, the social worker, was very approachable and sensitive to our needs. We participated in a deeply comprehensive review process that included individual interviews as well as home visits. We initially wanted a baby boy younger than Bernard. The Northhaven agency registered our name with their network of adoption agencies in five states: Ohio, Pennsylvania, Connecticut, Massachusetts, and New York. We were advised that due to New York's liberal abortion policy and because many unwed mothers were beginning to keep their babies without disabilities, it would be difficult to locate a baby within months. We told the social worker that we would consider a deaf baby boy. That helped speed up the search process that otherwise would have taken three to five years.

Fifteen months later, in May 1975, Anne Lane informed us that a fifteen-month-old hard of hearing baby girl, Stephanie Diane Clark, was available through an adoption agency, the Jewish Family and Children's Service in Boston. A girl? They mailed us a photograph of her, a pudgy and beautiful little toddler. We were immediately smitten.

"Would you like to have a sister?" we asked Bernard. We'd always planned that we'd adopt a boy.

"Sure," he said easily. "I just want someone to play with. I want to meet her!" Maybe we would get our Stephanie after all.

We were initially advised to plan a few trips to Boston to first meet with the social worker and the foster mother with whom Stephanie lived. We were at first disappointed because we'd imagined bringing her home right away. But the agency wanted to be sure that we would be the right fit for her. At that time, we had plans to drive to Maryland, where I would participate with the Rochester bowling team in the Eastern Deaf Bowlers Association tournament. To kill two birds with one stone, we added the Boston trip after the bowling tournament. Bernard rode with us as we drove to Stamford, Connecticut, to visit our friends Louis and Doris Blanchard, and then we stayed overnight at Richard and Arlene Thompson's home in Boston.

The next morning, it was pouring rain. The three of us, Vicki, Bernard, and I, dashed through the downpour into the adoption agency to meet with another social worker, Ruth Wolf.

"Would you like to meet Mary Nickerson and the baby?" Ruth asked us, taking our wet coats and hanging them up on a hook by the door. Yes, we would! She walked us down a long hallway and into a room, where we saw Mary, the foster mother, and a sixteen-month-old Stephanie Diane, the chubby toddler from our photograph. As soon as we entered the room, we were mesmerized by Stephanie. She looked up at us from the floor where she sat playing with toys, her long eyelashes fluttering. We all sat on the floor with her. I could tell that Bernard liked her immediately. We were all in love. The baby reached for the comb peeking out of my front shirt pocket and pulled it out, fascinated. We spent about an hour with her while her foster mother and the social worker looked on. Vicki, smiling joyfully as she watched Stephanie stare at Bernard and me, said, "I think she prefers males!"

"I know this isn't planned, but do you think you could stay an extra night?" Ruth asked us in her office afterward. Surprised, we asked why.

"I think Mary was so impressed with you that she might be ready to let you take Stephanie home tomorrow."

I glanced over at Vicki and saw the love and excitement in her face that must have been mirrored on mine. "Yes, yes!" we told Ruth. "We will stay another night."

Ruth drove us around Boston and to lunch. This gave us a chance to learn, though not as much as we hoped, about Stephanie's family and medical history. Her biological mother was fifteen and Jewish, her father Catholic and twenty-seven. Her mother was an A student and athletic, and she called every single day to check if Stephanie had been placed with adoptive parents yet. "The calls will stop if you take Stephanie home," Ruth said with a smile.

That night, we stayed in a motel, but it was hard to sleep because of the excitement. Would we really be driving back home to Rochester with a daughter? We met Ruth in front of Mary's house in Newton. She was holding Stephanie, who was dressed in a warm jacket, her bag packed. Ruth handed Stephanie into Vicki's arms. "Enjoy her!" she told us.

Bernard sat up in the front seat with me so that Vicki could hold Stephanie on her lap in the back seat (car seats for children were not required at that time). Stephanie was not receptive to being hugged, maybe because Mary had avoided hugging Stephanie, knowing she would eventually be adopted. But she was comfortable sitting on Vicki's lap.

We believe our daughter was meant for us, so we kept her first name and replaced her middle name with Vera. In a naming ceremony at Temple Sinai, she was blessed with a Hebrew name, Sarah Hadassah. We didn't know at the time, but we later learned that Mary's husband's name was Bernard, and also that we had started our adoption process on the very same day Stephanie was born—January 5, 1974.

On the trip home, Vicki looked through Stephanie's bag of clothes and found a note from Mary describing Stephanie's affinity for certain foods, especially egg salad sandwiches, which she won't eat today as an adult. The bag included a long strip of lollipops, which Vicki thought were for Bernard. Since he never cared for candy, she put them away.

We learned later that Stephanie was Mary's one-hundredth foster baby. When Mary noticed Stephanie didn't babble like the other babies, she kept her longer than she usually kept a baby in her care. When Stephanie was five months old, Mary had her hearing tested and was told she was "hard of hearing." The baby was fitted with two behind-the-ear hearing aids; then, when Stephanie was fifteen months old, Mary felt that Stephanie was ready for adoption. Later, Mary told us she was very fond of Stephanie. We kept in touch with Mary every year until 2016 when she passed away. We miss her letters.

In Stephanie's first few days at home with us, she did not seem to possess any language or communication skills. Her room was between ours and Bernard's, and Vicki and I would take turns sitting with her in the rocking chair next to her crib and reading her bedtime books each night, which she seemed to love. But she did not crawl, stand, or walk, nor was she weaned from a bottle. Stephanie sat cross-legged on the floor and moved around sideways. One of the pictures Mary sent us showed Stephanie sitting in a playpen, which made us realize the reason she hadn't learned how to crawl or walk before she came home with us was that she likely spent most of her time in a playpen in foster care. We taught her to crawl, and shortly afterward, she started walking and became active. A few weeks later, we went on a camping trip, where she was easily weaned from a bottle when we gave her a cup to drink from instead. She liked that better!

WE QUICKLY MADE arrangements to have Stephanie's hearing tested at the Rochester School for the Deaf (RSD), where we knew she would get her education. She was indeed profoundly deaf and fitted instead with two body aids. When behind-the-ear hearing aids became more robust, she wore them and still does today. Vicki and Stephanie joined the Demonstration Home Program, later the Parent-Infant Program, on the second floor of Perkins Hall in the administration building at RSD.

We often visited with our friends Harry and Pat Scofield and their two adopted sons, who were our children's playmates. One day, when

Stephanie was two, Pat gave lollipops to the boys but not to Stephanie since she knew Vicki never gave candy to our children. Catching sight of the lollipops, Stephanie's eyes lit up, and she cried out for one passionately. It was then that Vicki realized the long strip of lollipops Mary had put in the bag had actually been for Stephanie. "OK," Vicki said, "Just one!" Stephanie was thrilled and immediately stuck the red candy into her mouth. To this day, Stephanie continues to have a very sweet tooth.

Because of our strong oral upbringings, we decided that Stephanie would begin with an oral education, but she did not make any progress after a few days of us trying it. We realized that because she'd missed early language stimulation, we'd have to try a different approach. Immediately, we used clear sign concepts with spoken words to facilitate her language acquisition and comprehension. She quickly became responsive to sign language. Her first sign was "book," as she gently flipped the pages of a book. She was always fascinated with turning pages in books, magazines, and newspapers. Before long, she'd learned her ABCs, fingerspelling, and sign language, always cheerful and happy to learn new things. While she developed the vocabulary to communicate her ideas and needs to us, she used her voice, too. And lipreading came easy to her.

There's a saying that if children see a lot of books around their house, the chances are very likely they will become voracious readers, but this wasn't the case with Stephanie. No matter how much we tried to encourage her to read, she was not as interested in reading as Bernard had been at that age. She would read when and what she wanted to. She enjoyed comics and picture stories. That also went for writing—she'd only write when she wanted to, not on command. She wrote well enough to be understood, and that was good enough for her.

After Stephanie completed the Home Demonstration Program, she attended a preschool program at RSD and then School Number One, which is a public school with self-contained classes for deaf and hard of hearing students. She had a wonderful kindergarten teacher, Mrs. Charis Davis, but she had a personality clash with her first-grade teacher, who sent Stephanie to the principal's office so many times that we lost count. The principal often called us to come and pick up

Bernard and Stephanie as youngsters.

Stephanie. When Vicki learned that Stephanie was left to play in the area outside the principal's office while she waited for us to arrive, instead of being made to work on schoolwork, Vicki felt this was the wrong tactic to teach behavioral expectations.

"Of course, she doesn't mind being sent to his office," Vicki said. "It means playtime!"

One day in the fall, Stephanie came home after school crying.

"Oh no, what's wrong?" Vicki asked her.

Stephanie opened her backpack and pulled out a piece of paper, which she handed to Vicki. On the paper, a worksheet they'd done in her first-grade class that day, Stephanie's teacher had drawn a red sad-looking face. Stephanie was distraught. Was her teacher sad? Was she mad? Had she done something very wrong?

Full communication was what Stephanie needed, and the teacher had used a drawing without talking with her directly. Vicki called the teacher and objected. Later, when we met with the principal and the teacher, the principal complained to us that Stephanie had a strong personality and was causing trouble in her classes by being inattentive. Vicki and I looked at each other, and Vicki asked, "Because she's a girl, shouldn't she be strong and speak up for herself?" The principal looked so embarrassed. He coughed and shuffled some papers on his desk. He said nothing more about Stephanie's strong personality.

Vicki enjoyed being a homemaker, especially after having been a full-time volunteer for so many years in St. Louis. I knew that she had the potential to succeed in a college environment, and at RIT, she would have full communication access in all her classes, including interpreters that she never had in the past. At the time, we had become close friends with Joan Dickson while she was a part-time student at both RIT and the University of Rochester. She also worked full-time at RIT and had two young daughters. When I learned that Joan was planning to register for a course in adolescent psychology, I asked her to subtly encourage Vicki to take the course with her. But Vicki said, "No way!" when Joan asked her to join her in class. After she told me what Joan said, I asked, "Why not? You have nothing to lose by checking to see whether you like it or not. If not, then you can always withdraw."

Convinced, Vicki registered for the course as a special student. She was amazed by how much fun she was having in the class and enjoyed studying with Joan. Vicki was also blown away by her first experience of having an interpreter in the classroom. The top-notch sign language interpreter was Alice Beardsley, who happened to be hard of hearing. Vicki finally understood and enjoyed the class lectures, and with the interpreter, Vicki could participate in the class. She also realized how much information she had missed in high school and her previous colleges.

While she enjoyed interacting with the students and talking with the professor, she didn't want to continue school. She wanted to focus on Bernard's educational needs and continue as a homemaker. A few years later, while our children were in school, she applied for a major in office management at NTID but withdrew after taking a few courses that she didn't find challenging enough. Harriette Royer, a friend who happened to be a vocational rehabilitation counselor, offered Vicki a job tutoring an RSD student for a few hours each week.

In 1978, I was an active NAD member, and Alice Beardsley and I co-chaired the NAD conference in Rochester. We were fortunate to have an excellent mentor, Frederick C. Schreiber, then the NAD executive director, who came to Rochester almost every month for eighteen months to assist us with the conference planning. When Alice, unfortunately, had a heart attack that disabled her most of the year before the conference, I took over as the acting chair. Once Alice recovered in time to assume the chair role during the conference, I focused on the details of the conference's programs and activities. We were thrilled when Fred informed us that Rochester had broken the record for the largest conference attendance, with over 1,200 people. Vicki was the registration chair, and she coordinated a team of wonderful volunteers. She was very organized and prompt with her timelines, and Marv Sachs, the mathematics department chair at NTID, approached me after seeing how well Vicki handled the registration. He asked whether Vicki would be interested in working for him part-time as a records supervisor in the mathematics department. I told him to ask Vicki, and Vicki was so surprised as she shared the good news with me. I encouraged her to accept the job offer.

She enjoyed working part-time in the Math Learning Center and had a wonderful mentor, Dr. Marilu Raman, who at that time was acting chair while Mr. Sachs was on sabbatical. Dr. Raman was an excellent role model and encouraged Vicki to return to school.

Vicki's work experience influenced her to go back to school when she realized that although she enjoyed working, she didn't want to continue doing office work. She returned to major in social work on a part-time basis at RIT, while continuing to work part-time. Eventually, she left her job to study full-time and graduated with high honors and a bachelor's degree in social work at the age of thirty-nine.

As a social work student, Vicki performed her internship with the Rochester Mental Health Chapter under the supervision of Harriette Royer, then the director within The Health Association of Rochester. Harriette and Vicki were instrumental in developing a survey of the needs of deaf and hard of hearing children for a residential treatment facility (RTF), which led to the establishment of an RTF program for deaf and hard of hearing clients at Hillside Children's Center in 1983. Soon after her internship with Ms. Royer, the program at Hillside

Children's Center was up and running for deaf and hard of hearing clients. Vicki was involved with this without knowing our daughter would later need this kind of support during her years at RSD.

Vicki wanted to be home when our children were home from school, so she worked part-time as a coordinator for the Friendship through Sign Language program for the Monroe County Association for the Hearing Impaired at the Rochester Health Association. She was responsible for matching a hearing person aspiring to develop sign skills with a deaf adult with special needs who felt isolated at home. The goal was twofold: develop the hearing person's signing fluency while satisfying the deaf adult's socialization needs.

14

Advocacy for Access

I WAS LOVING ROCHESTER. Our house, which we'd found at the beginning of our second year in the city, was back in that first subdivision we'd liked from the start, the Village Green in Penfield, even though it was farther from my work than our first apartment.

When we'd first moved to Rochester in 1970, I became closely acquainted with Alice Beardsley, a seasoned leader of the Rochester Civic Association of the Deaf (RCAD) and the Empire State Association of the Deaf (ESAD) (which is an affiliate of the NAD). While Alice served two terms as ESAD president, she chaired the New York State Temporary Commission for Deaf and Hard of Hearing Individuals. I was in awe of Alice, who had grace and was always cheerful with a radiant smile. She was an excellent leader who worked well with her colleagues and influenced people to do their parts. She was well connected to legislators, state agency officials, and other politicians.

As a young member of the NTID faculty, I was very eager to become involved in community activities. Alice encouraged me to participate in RCAD and ESAD activities. She also accompanied me to my first RCAD meeting.

I was sitting next to her when the RCAD secretary, Claude Samuelson, began reading the meeting minutes to the membership. He had one hand in his pocket and used his other hand to fingerspell all of the minutes without moving his lips or using any facial/body expressions.

Vicki and I on the ESAD convention planning committee.

I stood there in amazement; I had never seen such rapid fingerspelling, nor someone fingerspelling an entire presentation. I couldn't understand him and looked helplessly at Alice. She laughed and interpreted the entire text in sign language for me. "How in the world can you understand him?" I asked. She said, "I'm used to him. I'm sure you'll pick it up with time," she assured me. She was right. After attending a few meetings and conversing with the secretary, I got accustomed to it. I later learned that Claude and Alice had attended RSD, which used fingerspelling and oral speech as their primary method of communication and teaching, thus giving the method its name: the Rochester Method. I'm forever grateful to Alice for introducing me to the Rochester Deaf community.

Over time, I became more actively involved in RCAD meetings, and I volunteered to serve on a committee. Eventually elected as the RCAD secretary, I represented the Rochester community at ESAD board meetings and conferences. Alice introduced me to outstanding leaders with the ESAD through its affiliations in Buffalo, Rochester, Syracuse, Rome, Utica, Binghamton, Albany, and New York City. We were engaged in a variety of legislative issues and made contacts with key legislators and state officials in Albany. We also worked with the commissioner of the New York State Temporary Commission for Deaf and Hard of Hearing Individuals.

Our mission was to help deaf people through advocacy for access to full participation in the larger society, including in education, technology, jobs, health care, and many other social realms. Oftentimes, we'd hold special events for the general population in local communities to increase awareness of the Deaf community, deaf people, and of ASL and Deaf culture.

One significant legislative bill among many was the Baby Bill, which was passed by the state legislators and signed into law by the governor. This law mandated that early hearing screening be administered to all newborns in hospitals in New York state.

LIFE WAS FULL! Stephanie was home with us, filling our house with more love and fun and conversation. Vicki was busy with the children, busy advocating and working for Deaf rights and services, and, as always, busy with house projects and with her many friends. For my part, I was busy making sure that the students at NTID, who by that year numbered around 650, were fully supported in their learning, in addition to all of my volunteer service with RCAD.

NTID had started in 1968 with seventy students. The plan was to add 100 new students each year until it reached a goal of 750 students. Later, when the rubella epidemic hit the United States in 1963, causing a surge of deaf babies called the "rubella bulge," NTID anticipated that there would be a corresponding increase of college-age students in the early 1980s, a prediction that proved right. In the 1980s, enrollment grew to over 1,400 students.

ONE DAY, Dr. E. Ross Stuckless, director for research at NTID, came to my office.

"Would you consider enrolling in a doctoral program in education at the University of Rochester?" he asked me. "If that sounds at all interesting to you, I'd like to introduce you to Dr. Jack Miller at the University of Rochester School of Education." Although I'd already been accepted into a doctoral program at Gallaudet, the idea of studying closer to home was more appealing, since we were still in the process of adopting our daughter. "Yes," I told Dr. Stuckless. "I'd love to meet with Dr. Miller to learn more." All told, four of us, all deaf NTID faculty members, met with Dr. Miller, who told us that if we applied, we'd be accepted.

My formal doctoral studies at the University of Rochester finally began in the fall of 1976. I was initially admitted to the educational psychology program. Though I enjoyed the program very much, after one year, I learned that none of the coursework I'd completed for my previous master's degree would be accepted. I would have to take additional courses outside of the program to earn my degree. I decided to transfer to the Curriculum and Teaching Department, with an emphasis in math and computer science education, and they accepted all of my previous master's coursework.

After one year of studying, Harry Lang and I were the only remaining deaf doctoral students. The other two had left for different reasons. Harry and I took a few courses together and so we shared interpreting services.

Kathy Gillies, the assigned interpreter, and I developed a strong bond as we worked closely with professors to ensure my full participation in the classes. Each class involved a group discussion with the professor speaking and allowing students to jump in with comments or questions. In the beginning, I felt lost because the professor talked too fast, and there was a lot of cross talk, which made it difficult for me to contribute. Kathy and I met with one professor and explained the problem. The professor agreed with us on a protocol: only one person would talk at a time; everyone would wait for the interpreter to finish interpreting (interpreters have to hear what the speaker said for a few seconds before beginning to interpret); and students should first raise their hands and wait to be called upon before speaking. It worked so well that Kathy and I worked with other professors using the newly adopted protocol.

Harry and I enrolled in an advanced statistics class taught by Jack Miller, who had proactively taken ASL classes so that he could communicate with us on a one-on-one basis. The day before our first class, he told us that he would sign for himself throughout the course because he felt that he had enough signing skills to teach the class. Harry and I exchanged a glance. It was clear to both of us that Dr. Miller's idea would be a disaster. We tried to talk him out of it, but Dr. Miller insisted, promising that if it didn't work out well, he would yield to the interpreter present in the class. Not only were we worried about understanding his signing, we were also concerned about how our hearing classmates would react to this plan. To our surprise, they agreed to it as an experiment.

Dr. Miller got through the entire semester on his own! Yes, he was still in the elementary stage of learning to use sign language, but he did his best to use proper signs and always asked for feedback. We could follow him because signing forced him to slow down so we could better read his lips while peripherally watching his signs, fingerspelling, facial expressions, and body language.

When we cautiously probed our hearing classmates about how they felt about Dr. Miller signing, we learned that they felt the same way we did: They appreciated how signing forced Dr. Miller to slow down and speak clearly. He made the class very interesting and fun—and we learned a great deal. We all got As.

Around this time, my mother told me via TTY that my father was very depressed and unhappy about his job at Metz Baking Company. This conglomerate bakery had purchased the smaller bakery where my father had worked for many years. Two years earlier, my mother explained to me, my father's supervisor had reassigned him to work at the dock, where he had to lift and move heavy baskets of bread and baked goods into trucks. My father had a long history of shoulder dislocations stemming from his sporting days at ISD, and so he asked to go back to his original job as a baker. The supervisor refused and laid him off. Naturally, my father was upset, but after several weeks, the supervisor called my parents' next-door neighbor to tell my father to return to work. Excited for the chance to work and earn money again, my father got up at 2 a.m. to be at work by 3 a.m. After a few days, though, he was once again laid off. This pattern, my mother told me, had continued for the next few months.

My father never understood what was going on. He tried to talk with the supervisor but was told that he was now a "jobber," which meant that he would be called in only when he was needed or as a substitute when other bakers took vacations or were out sick. My father lost all of his benefits—sick days, vacation days, and, most importantly, his pension. The jobber arrangement dragged on for the next two years, and this was hard on my parents financially. My mother continued to work, and my father would apply for unemployment benefits on the days he didn't go into work at the bakery.

That was the first time I'd heard about any of this, and I was horrified. I immediately flew to Sioux City to talk with my father. He tried to explain what happened, even though he didn't fully understand what was going on or why it had happened to him.

"Does your bakery have a union?" I asked him.

"Yes," he said.

"Have you ever talked with your union steward?"

"I don't know," he said, and I realized he wasn't sure what I was talking about.

"Have you ever seen any literature, any paperwork, about your union membership, Dad?" I asked him. Yes, there was a little booklet he had about the union. He retrieved it from a drawer in the kitchen, and I carefully studied the policies and procedures.

As I read, I realized that many of his rights as a union member had been violated and that something had to be done about it. I made an appointment with the union steward, and my father and I went downtown to meet with him. Before the meeting, I wrote down everything I wanted to cover. I described how the bakery had treated my father over the past two years and how they had violated his rights as a union member. The steward reviewed my father's case and was dumbfounded; he had not been aware of any of the incidents. He didn't like what he learned at all, so while we were still in his office, he called the company's corporate secretary and had a long talk.

The very next day, the union steward, my father, and I went to the corporate secretary's office. After another long talk, the corporate secretary called the supervisor into the office to inquire about my father's employment status. The supervisor didn't have a good explanation, so the corporate secretary reinstated my father as a "legitimate" and full-time baker. My father received back pay for the past two years, along with all of his accumulated sick and vacation days. His pension also was resurrected, and these two years were added to his years of employment. I knew my father was fortunate to have his job back, but I wondered how many other deaf people were in the same position without someone to help out. This incident instilled in me the importance of being sensitive and caring to all of the people with whom I worked and also the importance of fighting to secure rights for deaf workers.

IN THE FALL OF 1977, I was appointed as the NAD Region 1 Representative on the NAD Board of Directors. It was a wonderful experience being on a board with outstanding leaders from all over the United States. I was the official representative for thirteen northeastern state associations in my region, and I conducted regional meetings and workshops at regional conferences and during NAD conferences. I learned a great deal about the internal operations of the NAD, including its branch office in Indianapolis, which was operated by Gary W. Olsen. We grieved the former NAD executive director Frederick Schreiber's untimely death in the summer of 1979.

"Would you consider running for president?" the board asked me. We were in a small meeting room in Rochester, making preparations for the NAD centennial conference in Cincinnati, Ohio, in 1980. I had gotten to know many of these people well through my civic and advocacy work on local, state, and national levels. "I'd be grateful if you'd help me with my campaign then," I told Phil Bravin since we had already developed a close relationship through our involvement as board members and officers of the ESAD. Phil, who had a full head of thick, bright red fluffy hair and large square glasses, was a manager with IBM and a Gallaudet alumnus. He later went on to be one of only four deaf trustees on the Gallaudet College (later University) Board of Trustees during the tumultuous student protests in the late 1980s, when he stepped up as a much-needed liaison between the students and the university's administration. I had and continue to have tremendous respect for Phil as a humanitarian and a charismatic leader. I always enjoyed having deep and introspective chats with him about everything in life, our careers, and our families.

As soon as Phil agreed to become my campaign chair, we recruited wonderful volunteers who designed my campaign materials and developed campaign strategies. We sent campaign letters to all members of the NAD and all officers of affiliated state associations approximately nine months prior to the election at the conference. After we organized the campaign committee, I learned that a good friend of mine, Larry Forestal, had decided to run for the presidency as well. Regardless, we continued to remain friends throughout the campaign and after the election.

Our campaign committee members and volunteers worked hard for my candidacy. We produced follow-up letters, fliers, and posters throughout the week and hosted campaign parties each evening during the conference in Cincinnati. It was a very stressful time for both teams. Larry had many friends who attended Gallaudet College with him who supported him. Soon my team learned he also had several state association delegates committed to vote for him before the conference.

On our side, Phil and his committee lobbied the state association delegates to "de-commit" themselves and maintain an open mind about both candidates. Phil even encouraged some of the delegates to call their respective state association presidents/officers to seek their permission to de-commit. This way, they would be given the freedom to get to know both candidates before declaring their votes at the end of the week. Simultaneously, Phil and his team continued campaigning on my behalf with the remaining undecided delegates as well.

My platform was threefold. The highest priority was to continue to press CBS to caption TV programs during prime time. The other two priorities were creating a staff position for youth programs within the NAD and developing a coalition with national consumer and professional organizations serving deaf and hard of hearing people to advocate for human rights, ensure that jobs were available and accessible, and improve our quality of life. Larry's platform, to the best of my recollection, was focused primarily on enhancing educational opportunities for deaf students, protecting residential schools for deaf children, and preserving ASL and Deaf heritage, among other important topics.

Vicki and I were somewhat frustrated when we saw what we would call "dirty" politics, such as influencing, promising, misquoting or misrepresenting facts, and trading votes with and among the delegates. We quickly learned that it was a part of the game. However, it got so bad that by the middle of the week, I was somewhat disillusioned and seriously considered withdrawing. Thankfully, Phil persuaded me to stay on.

"We're making good progress with undecided delegates, Alan," he told me. "We'll get as many of them as we can to your evening parties, to give them a chance to get to know you. When they get to know you, they'll want to vote for you." At the parties, Phil and his team kept watch and told me to approach and strike up conversations with certain delegates. Phil advised me not to focus on persuading them, but rather on having good conversations with them about their issues, concerns, or thoughts. Vicki and I agreed to go along with the game plan. Vicki and Phil's wife, Judy, worked together at Kinko's to get peel-off tags printed with "Vote ALAN HURWITZ for President-Elect" distributed to delegates.

Larry and I agreed that no matter what happened, we'd stay friends throughout the campaign. If Larry won, then I'd go to him and give him a big hug and congratulate him. On the other hand, if I won, I'd make the first move to go to Larry and hug him and to encourage him to remain committed to NAD's mission. The night before the election, we found out Larry and his team had held a previctory party. That confidence worried me, but Phil told me not to sweat it, and we continued to host events and have conversations with everyone. I didn't know until after the election that Phil continued to work throughout that night.

The next morning during the election, one by one, the delegates were called to announce their votes for either candidate. My team's hard work paid off: I edged Larry out by just three votes. I learned later that the night before, I was down by three or four votes, but overnight, several delegates switched sides—seven of mine went to Larry, and thirteen of his came over to my side. I have no idea how it happened, but I give the credit to Phil and his committee for their

Vicki and I after I was elected president-elect of the NAD.

persistence and hard work. Immediately after the announcement was made, I walked over to Larry, and we both hugged each other. "Great campaign!" I said. "Please, Larry, come work with our team, will you?"

He agreed and kept his word. Two years later, while I was the governing president at the next conference in Baltimore, he ran again for president-elect and won. It was a bittersweet victory for him, but I was happy he won.

In 1880 in Cincinnati, the NAD formed as an advocacy organization for signing deaf people as a response to the Milan Congress that outright banned the use of sign language in educational settings. Up until 1968, the NAD president could run for an unlimited number of terms. After one president, Byron B. Burnes, served for eighteen years, a term limit was introduced, and the office of president-elect was created. Under the new system, the elected officer served on the board for six years—two years as president-elect, then two years as president, and finally two years as past president. This system continued until 1986 when the board changed the bylaws so that a person could serve three consecutive terms as president.

After my experience as president, I fully supported the change. As president-elect for the first two years of my six-year term, I had very little opportunity to engage in leadership activities. When my term as president commenced, I faced a significant turnover of board members due to term limits. It took me approximately six months to work with and get the board attuned to my vision and strategic plan for the remainder of my presidential term, but I discovered that there wasn't enough time for me to achieve all of my goals and priorities. With this experience, I realized the next president-elect needed to be well prepared in advance. During the last six months of my two-year term, I started to prepare Larry for his role as president.

We developed several important position papers related to the cochlear implant controversy, education of deaf and hard of hearing students, television captioning, and interpreting services during my presidency. I once again commissioned Phil Bravin to work with the CBS executives on the captioning of its prime time television programs—*Cagney and Lacey, Designing Women, Newhart, Magnum P.I.,* and so forth.

We also created a full-time director position to support all youth programs, including Junior NAD, Youth Leadership Camp, and Collegiate NAD. I traveled extensively to state association conferences and represented the NAD at several national meetings related to the education of deaf students, television captioning, interpreting evaluation and certifications, and other pertinent issues. I also represented the NAD at the World Federation of the Deaf Congress in Varna, Bulgaria. I wrote monthly articles for the NAD publications *The Deaf American* and the *NAD Broadcaster*. I was on a fast track since I knew that I'd have a very short time to produce results during my presidency. The last two years of my six-year term was somewhat quiet while I served in a consultant role to support Larry as the next president. Currently, I serve as president emeritus of the NAD, which is an honorary role awarded by the board to one of the past presidents, normally based on seniority.

THANKS TO A decoder attached to our television, we were excited to watch the few prime-time TV programs that were captioned, including the very funny *Three's Company*. One of our other early favorite programs was *Dynasty,* which was on Wednesday nights.

In 1981, I flew to Washington, DC, early on a Wednesday morning to meet with congressional staff members all day long. I made sure my flight would get me home in time to watch *Dynasty*. Back then, deaf people had such limited access to captioned entertainment that it was common for us to place a very high value on a TV show. I arrived at the airport on time only to find that the plane was overbooked, and I was bumped off and scheduled for a flight the next morning. What? I panicked and argued with the airline agent: "I must get home tonight!" I told her. "I need to be on this flight."

"All I can do," she told me, "is put you on a wait list with a lot of other people ahead of you, sir."

Thirty minutes later, I learned that I would definitely miss the flight, so I marched back to the agent at the counter.

"I must get on this plane. I am deaf and my wife is deaf and I have no way to contact my wife to explain. I'm concerned about my family!" Finally, my pleas were getting to her. "I can try one last time," she said.

She boarded the plane herself and asked if anyone would be willing to get off the flight in return for the reward of an additional flight at no cost. One passenger volunteered to get off, and I was allowed to take his seat. The plane left a bit late and arrived in Rochester barely in time for me to run to my car in the parking lot and speed home to watch *Dynasty*.

15

A Chance to Lead

As DIRECTOR OF THE Office of Support Services, my responsibilities continued to grow, and in 1978, I was appointed associate dean for educational support services. A few years earlier, I had hired Anna Witter Merithew from Atlanta to lead interpreting services and interpreter training, to take that work off my plate. She was a master interpreter, an experienced trainer of interpreters, and a proud Coda.

As the number of interpreters kept growing, I split the department into two units: the Department of Interpreting Services and the Department of Interpreter Training. Marilyn Mitchell, who was the coordinator of an interpreter outreach program in Louisiana, was hired to lead the interpreting services department while Anna continued to lead the interpreter training programs. Anna and I codeveloped a new associate's degree program for educational interpreters. The department, the college-wide curriculum committee, the university-wide curriculum committee, the deans and vice presidents, the university president, and finally, the RIT Board of Trustees all approved the curriculum proposal. Upon the board's approval, it went to the New York State Education Department for final approval and certification in 1981.

After I completed my coursework at the University of Rochester in two years, I started working on my doctoral dissertation. I was fortunate when Dr. Stuckless formed and facilitated a "nudge" group for faculty members working on their dissertations. We met weekly during lunchtime to discuss issues and concerns about our research efforts and share ideas. Dr. Stuckless was a wonderful and compassionate mentor to all of us. I completed the dissertation in November 1979 and received my doctorate in February 1980. My dissertation, "Comparative Analysis in Reverse Interpreting in Two Separate Languages—ASL and PSE," focused on factors that influenced voice interpreting from two different forms of sign languages, ASL and Pidgin Signed English (PSE), to spoken English. My friend Harry Scofield modeled all the signing for my research.

The doctoral degree did not make me one iota more intelligent, but it gave me the tools and expertise to conduct and analyze research and to problem solve. It has also provided me with access to many opportunities throughout my career.

I WILL NEVER FORGET one of my meetings with Dean Bishop. He wrote in one of my performance evaluations that I needed to be less preoccupied with how others perceived me and to "depersonalize" issues. He added that "perception is like a pothole; it can break a man's leg." I wasn't sure I understood what he meant.

In 1980, Dean Bishop left NTID to pursue new business opportunities. His replacement was a man who was known at his previous institution of higher learning as "the Hatchet Man." The rumor gained validity when, immediately upon his arrival at NTID, he made many changes and demoted several members of his administrative team without warning. He tried to be friendly, but it was hard for many of us to trust him. It seemed that he kept changing his comments and decisions.

The new dean had no previous experience with deaf education or with deaf and hard of hearing people. It was a difficult and trying time for my colleagues and me, who reported directly to him. After about three years, I went to Dr. Castle and told him about my frustration with the dean's leadership performance. I said that things were so bad, I was contemplating stepping down from my leadership role and even leaving NTID. For reasons I never found out, the dean was eventually dismissed.

Without engaging the NTID community in a national search process for a new dean, Dr. Castle appointed Dr. Jim DeCaro, who at that time was a faculty member and a school director, as the new dean. After an uproar by faculty and staff about the lack of a search process for a new dean, Jim immediately withdrew from deanship. He advised Dr. Castle to put together a formal national search process. Jim eventually applied, and nine months later, he was the unanimous choice to be the dean. I was thrilled with the decision, as I had always enjoyed working with him.

Dr. Castle appointed me as associate vice president for governmental and external relations while I kept my responsibilities as associate dean. This new role allowed me to travel to Washington, DC, with Dr. Castle and his executive assistant, Wendell "Gus" Thompson, to meet with congressional members and their key staff members about NTID's budgetary requirements. We also participated in congressional hearings with the Senate and House appropriation committees. Over time, to our dismay, both houses ceased their budget hearings because they found it to be cumbersome and needed the time and resources to focus on other priorities. Nevertheless, it gave us a chance to meet with each member and the chairs of both committees and subcommittees and their respective staff members individually to discuss NTID's needs.

In the late 1980s, when NTID was still in excellent fiscal shape, Dean DeCaro put together a new strategic planning committee. The new strategic plan eventually led to a comprehensive reorganization of NTID's administrative/leadership structure.

Simultaneously, seven centers were established, and search processes were created for new center directors. I was strongly encouraged to apply for one of the centers for baccalaureate and graduate programs that included RIT college-based support departments and educational access/support services—pretty much the same job as I did in the past. However, I wanted to expand my horizons and applied for the center for technical studies, which included teaching and curricula leading to associate degrees. To my disappointment, another internal candidate was selected.

After the seven center directors were appointed, Dean DeCaro immediately created two associate dean positions in the Office of the Dean: associate dean for academic administration and associate dean for student affairs. I was appointed to the latter, which allowed me to work closely with students. Dr. Christine Licata became the associate dean for academic administration. In 1993, we had a new team of the dean, two associate deans, and seven center directors. I continued my role as associate vice president for government and external relations, so I had a dual reporting relationship with both Dean DeCaro and Vice President Castle for several years.

As I PROGRESSED through various leadership roles at NTID, I was either invited or encouraged to apply for several positions outside NTID, and I followed up on some of them. Each time I applied for a job, I learned something new and sharpened my skills.

In the mid-1980s, I applied for a superintendent position at ISD, the school my father had graduated from in 1938. After the interview, I was not offered the job after being grouped in the lower four of the eight semifinalists who did not have any previous experience as a school superintendent. Dr. William Johnson, the hard of hearing superintendent of the Illinois School for the Deaf for the past twelve years, was ultimately selected. Coincidently, Bill Johnson's father and my father were schoolmates at ISD, and he had also become a baker as a result of learning the trade there.

Later, I was a finalist for the CEO position at the Lexington Center, where the Lexington School for the Deaf was situated, and underwent a full interview process. Shortly afterward, one of the hearing members of the Lexington board of directors who was on the search committee decided to become a candidate for the position. He had just left his job as vice president of one of the national banks in New York City. He served as a member of NTID's National Advisory Group and was a father of deaf twin sons who attended Lexington School and NTID. When he met with me in private, he persuaded me to withdraw my candidacy so he could have the job. Amused at his bold and entitled strategy to eliminate his competition before the decision was made, I advised him it would be best to leave the choice to the board.

When the board ultimately hired him as the new CEO, the Lexington community and members of the Deaf community in New York City held a protest because they'd hoped and expected that a deaf person would be selected. The media became involved, and several New York state legislators contacted the center for an explanation. After a few months of mounting pressure, he resigned. The Lexington School for the Deaf superintendent, Dr. Oscar Cohen, a Coda whom I deeply respect, was then appointed as the interim CEO of the Lexington Center. He eventually became the permanent CEO and continued as superintendent until his retirement.

In 1991, I was one of two finalists for the provost position at Gallaudet University during I. King Jordan's presidency. My experience going through the full interview process with the entire Gallaudet community was interesting. Vicki and I enjoyed a lovely lunch chat with the search committee, led by Jack Gannon, at one of the Faculty Row houses. One of the most memorable interviews was with the faculty senate led by Dr. William Marshall. I thought I did well and looked forward to working closely with President Jordan and his management team. The other finalist was an alumnus and a superintendent of a school for the deaf, Dr. Harvey J. Corson, who was ultimately selected. During this process, one of the alumni, Jack Levesque, a friend of mine, sent me an email stating that he thought I would make an excellent provost, but that his loyalty was with the other finalist, a Gallaudet alumnus. This was when I learned how vital a prior Gallaudet connection was during the search and selection process. I was disappointed that I was not selected.

In the mid-1990s, I was a finalist for the superintendent position of the North Carolina School for the Deaf in Morganton. After my interview with the search committee went well, I drove around and checked out the small town to be sure Vicki would be happy if we were to move there. I realized that it was not a viable place for my family—it was a very remote, though beautiful, area, so I withdrew my application. One of my friends, Gary Mowl, was ultimately selected as the new superintendent.

Going through these executive search processes helped prepare me for my subsequent interviews. After one of these interviews, the search committee chair, a man I'd known as a friendly acquaintance for several years, walked me out. "When you give such broad answers, you unknowingly waste some of your time telling them things other than what they are specifically searching to hear from you. In the future," he said kindly, "Stick to answering the questions they actually ask you."

In other words: I had talked too much. Unsurprisingly, I didn't get that job. But I'd learned a valuable lesson, and I would always be grateful for the chair's willingness to give me an honest critique.

I also learned that the best time to test the job market to see how marketable I was was when I was fully content with my work responsibilities.

Today, I often advise job seekers not to search for another opportunity nor test the market when they are unhappy with their employment. It is best to resolve any problems with your current situation before you start looking for other opportunities. I am often reminded of Abraham Lincoln's tough climb; before he became president, he lost fourteen previous elections for public office. With that in mind, the message is not to give up, and to continue to seek new opportunities throughout your career.

In 1994, after Dr. Castle retired from the college, Dean DeCaro became the interim director of NTID. A national search for a new RIT vice president and NTID director began in 1995. Dr. Robert R. Davila and I were the two finalists. Dr. Davila was the headmaster/superintendent of the New York School for the Deaf (Fanwood) in White Plains, New York. Before his appointment to Fanwood, he had been the assistant secretary for the Office of Special Education and Rehabilitative Services within the US Department of Education during President George H. W. Bush's administration. Before that, he'd been vice president for precollege programs at Gallaudet.

Although I didn't plan to apply for the position, I was encouraged by the search committee to do so. I didn't know at the time that Dr. Davila would apply for the post. Had I known he was seriously considering it, I would not have applied. Nevertheless, it gave me another unique experience of going through a search process. Davila got the job, making him the first Deaf Latino chief executive officer of the institute. RIT President Albert J. Simone told me that although I was a strong candidate, he believed that Dr. Davila was a better fit for the position. I told him that I would be happy to support Dr. Davila in whatever way I could. Davila began his term on July 1, 1996. In 1998, following a national search, I was selected as the dean of NTID.

MY MOTHER HAD a serious heart condition since she was in her fifties, and had a quadruple bypass heart surgery at the age of sixty-nine while I was at NTID. Since the operation was not successful, she struggled with her health for the next seven years. Fortunately, she saw me obtain my doctoral degree from the University of Rochester. On November 25, 1995, she passed away in Kansas City at the age of seventy-five.

My father continued to live alone at home and didn't want to move elsewhere. After a bad fall on black ice, while picking up a newspaper on his driveway, he developed ulcers. At the time, he wouldn't accept my suggestion that he move to Rochester so that I could help out. Fortunately, his doctor and also our friend, Merle Reekers, encouraged him to move. Finally, in February 1996, my father agreed to move to our home for a month until we found an apartment for him. I used Merle's son Scott's truck to haul a small moving trailer with my father's furniture and other belongings. Scott, an NTID student, then drove my father's car to Rochester. Having my father in Rochester allowed me to take him out every week for lunch, to the grocery store and the cleaners, and to see his doctors. Each time I drove his car, I asked him if he wanted to drive, but he refused. A year later, when his driver's license and insurance expired, he decided not to renew them. We donated my father's car to a charitable organization. He enjoyed having visits from us and would come to our home for holidays and celebratory meals. Four years later, he passed away on February 17, 2000. He was buried next to my mother in Kansas City.

Shortly afterward, my paternal Aunt Cranie moved from St. Louis to the same apartment building where my father lived. Vicki and I took care of Aunt Cranie for the next four years before she passed away. She was buried with her husband, Max, in Cleveland, Ohio.

When Dr. Davila announced his intention to retire from RIT/NTID in 2005, RIT President Simone decided to combine two executive positions—Davila's vice president position and my position as dean of NTID—into a single job. NTID was too small, Dr. Simone believed, to justify two separate executive positions.

Of course, this impacted me both personally and professionally: I might find myself very soon out of a job. You would think since I was already the dean, it would seem logical to allow me to assume the newly combined position. Not a chance. Though I thought it was strange for Dr. Simone to make this decision without discussing it with me first, I respected his position. It was his call to make.

He wanted a national search, but he encouraged me to apply for the position if I wanted it. Not clearly understanding his motive, I decided not to because I was not sure if he wanted me in this role. When the search committee eventually invited me to apply, I consulted with my trusted colleagues and family. They convinced me that I could be an effective leader of NTID at RIT. With much hesitancy, I sent my application to the committee. Weeks later, I found out that I was one of four finalists. We went through an intensive interview process spanning weeks.

A few months later, while I was holding my breath, wondering if I had the job, I attended one of the biweekly breakfast seminars at the president's house. Muffins, donuts, and fruit were laid out on a large side table, as usual, flanked by urns of hot coffee. "Dr. Hurwitz," Dr. Simone said, "Please come see me in my office later this afternoon if you don't mind."

"Well," I thought to myself, "He is going to inform me that I didn't get the job." I started to think of Plan B, Plan C, and more for my future. That afternoon, Dr. Simone had the pained look of a stern person trying to be friendly. I sat across from him and an interpreter at a round table. When he said he had five tough questions for me as a part of his final interview with me, I told him to go ahead. They were thought-provoking and intriguing questions to which I answered the best I could. They were related to my leadership style, personality, philosophy of higher education, management skills, and long-term goals for NTID and RIT.

After about an hour, he put his hands above the table and then signed to me, "The job is yours." I was flabbergasted and stunned, which might have shown on my face.

"Are you surprised?" he asked me.

"Yes," I told him. "I was preparing myself for the worst." He smiled and said I did very well in the other interviews. He admitted he wasn't at first sure how well I would do with my presentation after he saw the three other candidates' excellent performances. I was the last finalist to present to the entire NTID community. Fortunately, my presentation made him confident I would make a good leader.

"Could you keep the news quiet for another eight days, since Dr. Davila is out of the country in Japan?" he asked me. Of course, I could. He wanted Dr. Davila to be present when he announced the final decision to the NTID community. With a knowing smile on his face, Dr. Simone added, "But you can tell your wife. Nobody else, though; just her."

I returned to my office and continued to work as if nothing out of the ordinary had happened. Lin Hoke, my administrative assistant, knowing that I'd had an appointment with Dr. Simone earlier, lingered in my doorway as if waiting for me to say something. I could tell she was afraid to ask me and might have thought to herself that I was not selected.

I called Vicki via videophone to let her know the good news and told her to keep it mum for the next eight days. It was hard, believe me. Everywhere I went, people stared at me with concern, and Vicki was uncomfortable having to respond to friends that she didn't know whether I got the job. I hope they've forgiven her for the white lie!

Dr. Simone sent out a notice that he would be making an announcement the following week in the Panara Theatre—and offered no more detail. Rumors were flying around like crazy. Looking back, I must admit it was fun to see people making wild guesses about who got the job. Even so, it was a difficult time for Vicki and me while we sat separately in the audience; she sat with the student life team.

Finally, Dr. Simone made the announcement at the podium. I was prepared for the worst from the audience because I wasn't sure what they expected. They jumped up and waved their hands as I went to the stage to be greeted by Dr. Simone and Dr. Davila. Unbeknown to me, our children and grandchildren were waiting outside the theater until the announcement was made. I was surprised when Vicki led them inside to celebrate my new appointment.

In hindsight, I am glad Dr. Simone made the wise decision to go with a national search and that I went through the rigorous application and interview process. If it weren't for the national search—had I simply been promoted to that position—others would likely have questioned whether it was a fair process, thus making my job more difficult.

On December 1, 2003, I began my new responsibilities as the first chief executive officer who had been born deaf. Dr. Davila, who had become deaf at the age of eleven due to spinal meningitis, was given a six-month sabbatical leave and an office on campus for his external work with his colleague at the National University in San Diego. It was good to have him around, so that I could consult with him when I needed to. He was a great mentor and a good friend, and I deeply appreciated his wisdom.

As soon as I began my new role as vice president and dean, I determined that it was time to take another hard look at the structure of the Office of the Dean. The seven-center structure didn't live up to its potential, in my view. While it was meant to establish seamless collaboration, each center was too preoccupied with its own internal operations to collaborate. On top of that, there were some turf-related tensions among the centers. The concept of a flat organizational hierarchy had some merit, but the directors' personalities likely prevented them from working harmoniously together. Departments with similar academic disciplines were not collaborating, making it complicated for students to enjoy frictionless transfers from one academic program to another across the centers.

After discussing my concerns with key individuals at the college, including President Simone and Provost McKenzie, I dissolved the center structure. I then merged departments with similar disciplines into a single academic department. The new academic departments would then report directly to a new associate vice president for academic affairs. Naturally, establishing principles, guidelines, and timelines to restructure and merge the departments took some time. I drafted a paper, "Shaping and Sharing Our Future," which incorporated a shared

Al and Carolie Simone and myself.

vision, principles, and guidelines for reorganizing the structure. We then shared it with the community for their input and feedback. The response was mixed, though mostly positive; some folks were concerned about the implementation details. I knew that change was not easy for some people in the community, but it was time for a new direction that would best serve the interests of students and the college. When I appointed individuals to serve in key leadership positions in the new structure, I believed we had a dream team. We then moved forward to achieve many strategic goals.

In one of my meetings with President Simone, when I was RIT dean and vice president for NTID while discussing my annual appraisal, he shared comments that touched me. "I'm impressed, Alan!" he said. "You're running a smooth operation, and I admit that at first, I wasn't sure you were up to the job, but now I see that I was wrong to doubt you." He summed it all up by saying, "Folks *had* to work for the previous vice president, but with you, folks *wanted* to work for you!" I still remember to this day how kind he was to me and how much encouragement from a boss could mean to employees at any level in a workplace. Inspired by his example, I have tried to provide the same support to my employees.

When Dr. Simone decided to retire after fifteen years, a national search for a new RIT president commenced. Dr. William W. Destler was hired as the new RIT president on July 1, 1997, coming from the University of Maryland in College Park, where he was provost, department chair, dean, and vice president for research. He was also a successful fundraiser for the university. Being an electrical engineer professor himself, he and I connected well. After working closely with him for a year, he bestowed upon me a new title as the president of NTID while retaining my title as RIT vice president and dean. It was a new beginning for NTID and showed that RIT had enormous respect for NTID.

Later in 2008, when President William W. Destler hired Dr. Jeremy Haefner as the new provost at RIT, he needed to find someone to become his associate provost for academic affairs for RIT. Since Dr. Licata, who served as associate vice president for academic affairs at NTID, was highly recommended by the former provost and other academic leaders on the RIT side, Dr. Haefner approached me about Dr. Licata's appointment as a possible associate provost. Although I was hesitant at the idea of losing Dr. Licata, I believed that it would be a good move not only for her but also beneficial to have someone very knowledgeable about NTID in the Office of the Provost. Dr. Licata had been one of my closest and trusted colleagues for the past ten years during my deanship and presidency. Every time she entered a room, she lit it up like sunshine, with her cheerfulness and optimism. She'd done an excellent job grooming Dr. Laurie Brewer, her associate vice president for academic administration, for advancement into a senior leadership position. Dr. Brewer easily stepped in as the new associate vice president for academic affairs for NTID. Ultimately, it was a smooth transition for both NTID and the provost.

I established a new committee with Dr. Jeff Porter, the center director for research, to help us to develop the Strategic Vision 2010 (SV2010). The SV2010 served as a guide for our administrative and

With Bill Destler after being named president of NTID.

leadership teams. It was one of my first initiatives, assessing where NTID should be headed in the next five to ten years.

We identified four goals. First, we wanted to offer three distinct areas of study in career-focused degrees (associate's degrees), transfer degrees (associate's degrees), and baccalaureate and master's degrees. Second, we would establish formal referral programs with selected community colleges to prepare students for their eventual admission to NTID. Third, we would expand access services to meet the changing needs of our cross-registered students in the other colleges of RIT. And last but not least, we would develop an educational outreach consortium to share our expertise with others to improve the education and career development of individuals who were deaf or hard of hearing. The administrative team, in collaboration with the department heads, faculty, and staff, implemented the initiatives from the SV2010. These initiatives reflected bold and significant changes to NTID's academic programs, access services, and outreach efforts to more closely align with the needs of deaf and hard of hearing students.

We launched a new associate of science degree, which was a fast-track transfer degree program similar to 2+2 or 2+3 programs in broad areas that matched RIT offerings in the undergraduate programs. This would prepare students for their future careers, including fields in the humanities, such as journalism and international development. We realigned academic departments to allow faculty and staff with similar backgrounds and training to provide seamless guidance and support to students who aspired to transfer from associate degree programs to baccalaureate programs.

For students who weren't academically ready for NTID yet, we developed referral programs. NTID also worked closely with selected community colleges to create college-readiness programs that emphasized reading and writing, math, career awareness, and interpersonal growth through the efforts of the Northeast Technical Assistance (NE-TAC) and Postsecondary Education Programs Network (PEPNet). We expanded access services to meet the changing needs of deaf and hard of hearing students in seven other colleges of RIT.

We also made investments in new technology, and we researched the effectiveness of various access services, including C-Print (real-time captioning) services, hearing aid technology, and support for students with cochlear implants. We spearheaded the formation of an educational outreach consortium to share its expertise with others and to improve deaf and hard of hearing people's education and career development.

We oversaw the creation of a total of seven outreach programs for deaf and hard of hearing youth in grades seven to eleven—great programs like Math Counts, Tech Girlz, and the National Science Fair, in addition to NTID's traditional Explore Your Future program.

And near to my heart was our work to establish the Center of Excellence for the Study of Sign Language Interpreting, to understand better how interpreting affects learning and to determine what factors were related to interpreting comprehension, knowledge, and access.

NTID received $600,000 from the Johnson Scholarship Foundation to create a matching fund with the federal government for a $1.2 million scholarship fund, which would provide opportunities for deaf and hard of hearing students eager to become successful entrepreneurs.

As a result of these accomplishments, I traveled to Washington, DC, on behalf of RIT/NTID, to accept the New Freedom Initiative Award from US Department of Labor Secretary Elaine L. Chao in recognition of NTID's work in furthering educational and employment opportunities for deaf and hard of hearing individuals.

In my second year as RIT vice president and NTID dean, my loyal executive assistant, Gus Thompson, retired. I hired one of my closest and trusted colleagues, Don Beil, to fill the role. Don had a stellar thirty-five years of experience as a professor of computer science and, in 1996, was chosen to receive the RIT Eisenhart Award for Outstanding Teaching as Professor of the Year. He held several interim administrative positions as a department chair and school director. Don and I often traveled to Washington, DC, to meet with key congressional staff members and our colleagues, including critical liaisons between the US Department of Education and RIT/NTID. Don's primary responsibility was to coordinate meetings for the National Advisory Group, a required activity stipulated in the Education of the Deaf Act. This federal law specifies both NTID and Gallaudet University as specialized institutions for deaf and hard of hearing students.

THE COLLEGE OF LIBERAL ARTS dean at RIT made a strategic decision to dissolve the baccalaureate degree program in social work during the early 2000s. Since its inception in the 1970s as the only liberal arts major at RIT, the social work program had been a model for educating deaf and hard of hearing students alongside hearing RIT students—in fact, nearly half of the program's students were deaf. Many of NTID's alumni, including Vicki, had graduated from the program and gone on to have successful careers as outstanding leaders. Several professors learned sign language so that they could communicate with students in one-on-one situations. Interpreters and notetakers were in extensive use. It was a model, an example of what deaf/hearing education could look like.

But for several years leading up to the dean's decision to cut it, the social work program had faced a declining enrollment of hearing students. They could go to other local colleges with lower tuition to study social work, such as the State University of New York at

Brockport and Nazareth College. At the same time, the RIT College of Liberal Arts expanded its program offerings into many new majors, giving both deaf and hearing students multiple choices of programs other than social work.

The dean approached me to explore the possibility of transferring the social work program to NTID. I agreed to give it serious consideration and deliberated with my administrative team and the RIT provost.

The social work program was accredited by the Council of Social Work Education (CSWE), which is recognized by the Council for Higher Education Accreditation as the sole accrediting body for social work programs in the nation. We decided to check its accreditation requirements and realized that CSWE required that each social work program maintain a minimum of five full-time certified professors with doctoral degrees in the same discipline. I went back to the dean to inform him that we would be interested in this concept, provided that he agree to transfer his faculty to NTID at their cost, or at least share the cost with NTID. No, he explained, it would be our responsibility to fully cover the cost without the help of any resources from RIT. That meant we would have to decide to reallocate NTID's internal resources, yet we were not prepared to do this. I checked with the senior staff at the US Office of Special Education and Rehabilitative Services (OSERS) to see if we could increase NTID's budget to support the social work program. They denied our request because they viewed it as a duplication of efforts with Gallaudet University, which already had undergraduate and graduate programs in social work. The OSERS discourages both institutions of higher education—Gallaudet University and NTID—to duplicate academic programs, especially when using federal funds. I went back to the dean to inform him that NTID was unable to accept his proposal without financial support from the university.

This situation was a massive disappointment to the entire social work program and to me. Students, alumni, and faculty were understandably disillusioned with the decision and bombarded us with letters of protest. To this day, alumni from the social work program continue to meet during RIT/NTID's special events and reunions, most recently at NTID's fiftieth anniversary celebration. I understand their desire to bring the social work program (or its equivalent) back and believe that it could become a possibility under different circum stances.

One of the highlights during my tenure as the leader of NTID was to acquire $2 million from Communication Services for the Deaf (CSD) to construct a new student development center. CSD's generous contribution enabled NTID to build a $4.5 million, two-story, 30,000-square-foot building to extend students' learning experiences by fostering their potential for leadership and community service and to provide opportunities to explore other interests through nontraditional educational and recreational activities.

At the grand opening ceremony with CSD CEO Dr. Ben Soukup, RIT President Destler, and NTID Student Congress President Sarah Gordon, I was gratified that Dr. S. Richard Silverman's quote from the NTID dedication ceremony in 1974 was imprinted on the circular wall in the building: "NTID . . . shall be a lustrous beacon . . . of such magnitude, dignity, and decor . . . that will illuminate the hearts of all who come to be served here."

IN THE 1990s, I was faced with one of the most challenging issues at NTID when Deaf community members criticized the fact that one of our dorms was named after Alexander Graham Bell. Bell's longstanding philosophy of oralism as the primary means for educating deaf children and his involvement with eugenics led him to discourage deaf adults from marrying other deaf adults to prevent future births of deaf children. In the late 1970s, when these new NTID buildings were constructed, the administration chose the building names in the complex. At that time, the administration thought Bell was a fair choice because one of the other buildings had been named after Peter N. Peterson, a deaf teacher at the Minnesota Academy/School for the Deaf, who had visualized a National Technical Institute for the Deaf in an article in 1934. Even though the Deaf community had previously brought this injustice to the attention of the past chief executive officers, the name Bell remained.

With the advent of social media, conversations became more heated and more public. Students, faculty, staff, and alumni became engaged in difficult discussions with the administration, demanding that the name be removed. When I became dean in 1998 and then chief executive officer of NTID in 2003, this matter became a much larger issue to the point that the RIT administration and the board of trustees requested that I address it appropriately.

I appointed a committee of deaf, hard of hearing, and hearing students, faculty, and staff with an inclusive balance of differing perspectives and asked Jim DeCaro to lead the committee. After several weeks of deliberating, the committee had come to a determination of no consensus. The committee subsequently recommended that the name remain on the building, and the wordings on the plaque be modified to incorporate the historical perspective, including the issues and concerns related to language and communication raised by the Deaf community. Believing this was a reasonable approach, I decided to move forward with the committee's recommendation.

When some members of the committee dissented with the final recommendation by starting the protest again, comments were posted and widely distributed on social media around the world. I was disappointed that the commenters did not respect the committee's recommendations, and the RIT president and the board of trustees were displeased with the reaction.

I subsequently held an open forum with the entire NTID community and asked for their input. A faculty member, who I deeply respected, stood up and said that she firmly disagreed with removing the name. However, she explained she believed that it was necessary to remove the name so that we could move forward with NTID's mission and attend to the pressing student needs, curriculum development, and teaching. I sensed that the majority at the forum were in agreement, so I recommended to President Destler that we remove the name. The trustees learned that A. G. Bell was no longer alive and that NTID had never received any monetary donations from the family nor the associated organization. As a result, they authorized the removal of the plaque and Bell's name.

I instructed the assistant vice president for the NTID facilities to handle the removal; the plaque was removed and, without my knowledge, melted. Several weeks later, a group of students who led the protest against the naming of the Bell Hall asked for the plaque. When

I asked them why, they said they wanted to celebrate the removal by throwing eggs, tomatoes, and more at it. I said, "Sorry, the plaque is gone and melted." They were so upset, they posted about it on social media afterward, and then it finally quieted down.

Instead of renaming the building, its name reverted to its original name of Building C. At the time of this book's writing, in 2020, there is an influx of other colleges and universities changing the names of their buildings. Interestingly, some universities and institutions are considering an "additive" approach by leaving the controversial monuments alone and adding other monuments in honor of women leaders and other leaders of racial and ethnic movements. Other universities are considering expanding the wordings on such monuments as a reflection of historical discrimination and oppression or even removing these monuments and placing them in a museum or the like.

16

Our Pop-Up Camper

BEING DEAF CAN CLOSE one off from some things—certain conversations, career paths, radio, and aspects of religious life. My grandfather—with his stern face and firm ideas inherited from his European Orthodox life—had discouraged both my father and me from being bar mitzvahed because he believed the Torah exempted deaf people. But when our son Bernard was born hard of hearing, Vicki and I couldn't do the same. We thought, "Why can't we at least *try* to give our son full entry into Judaism? Isn't that his birthright?"

Vicki and I encouraged Bernard to learn about Jewish rituals and prepare for his bar mitzvah. However, we were concerned that he would be disqualified in the end because he didn't regularly attend Sabbath services, which was a requirement for a bar mitzvah. While Bernard resisted going to temple services, he did attend Sunday School regularly.

"Should we force him to go to temple services?" we asked the rabbi.

"No," he said. "Don't make Bernard hate being a Jew! Why not try individual tutoring in Hebrew instead?"

Bernard often said he didn't want to continue with confirmation classes, but to our surprise, he changed his mind and made it through to the end. As I watched my son drape his tallit around his shoulders for the first time at his bar mitzvah service, I wished that my grandfather could be there to see him. Unfortunately, he'd died a few years before at the age of ninety-seven.

Realizing how much my son's bar mitzvah had meant to me, I myself was bar mitzvahed for the first time in my late sixties. Vicki and I were visiting Russia as part of a Postsecondary Education Network-International trip with my colleague Jim DeCaro, the project director. We met with the director of a postsecondary center for deaf and hard of hearing students, and she happened to be Jewish. She had a very close relationship with a rabbi in Kazan, so she brought us to meet with the rabbi and his wife in a private room at their temple. The rabbi asked if I had been bar mitzvahed, and I explained that my grandfather had emigrated from Russia back in the late 1890s, and he had exempted my father and me because of our being deaf.

"You should be bar mitzvahed right here and now," the rabbi surprised me by saying. I was stunned. Didn't it take many years of work to prepare for a bar mitzvah? The rabbi persuaded me to take advantage of his offer, and he said he would make it a simple procedure. Vicki and Jim both encouraged me to go through with it. I thought of Kirk Douglas, who was bar mitzvahed in his eighties. If he could do it, then I should do it. The rabbi took me, with my designated interpreter, to the synagogue and told me what we would do. Once we were ready, the rabbi told Vicki and Jim to come in to watch. It was an intriguing and exhilarating experience for me. I had finally had my bar mitzvah. I had wondered why my father and I were exempted, but then there was no opportunity for a deaf person to achieve this goal in the small town of Sioux City. Afterward, we celebrated with a large Russian dinner.

BERNARD TOOK REGULAR classes at public schools. He first attended a small private kindergarten; it didn't match his social, linguistic, and academic needs, so at the recommendation of a child psychologist, he began taking classes in a public school. He did not meet the entry criteria for decibel hearing loss for RSD. The New York State Department of Education had and continues to have an archaic policy that requires a child to have at least an 85-decibel hearing loss to be admitted into a school for the deaf in New York state.

I was bar mitzvahed a second time when Rabbi Yehoshua Soudakoff, who is deaf and the son of deaf parents whom we knew well, was on campus at Gallaudet for a visit. He came to my office for a chat and I told him about my experience being bar mitzvahed in Kazan, Russia. He offered to give me another blessing in a brief ceremony in my office.

Despite the frustrations we often felt when searching for the best educational and social match for Bernard, we were very proud of his academic accomplishments. Academically, the potential was there for him to do even better. Like many kids, however, he preferred to play Atari, work on his computer, listen to music, play baseball, collect baseball cards, write, and read, read, read. He was the editorial editor for his high school newspaper. Remembering how my mother used to "force" me to read books for at least one hour a day before I could go outside to play, I realized that Bernard was my opposite; we encouraged him to go out to play for at least an hour before he was allowed to come back inside the house to read a book.

A STEADY BREEZE cooled my face, and the sky above us was bright blue, but things were not going well. I looked over and saw that Harry was laughing at my repeated attempts to assemble the many aluminum poles, which I had to fit into each other, end to end. The idea was to create one long, flexible pole, which I would then feed into the canvas pockets at the corners of the tent.

"There's a trick to it," I told him laughingly.

"Aren't you an engineer?" he teased me. When I refused to answer, he added, still smiling, "*This* is why we have a camper."

Harry and Pat Scofield's pop-up camper, parked at the adjacent campground 200 feet away, contained two beds piled with blankets and soft pillows. It was attached to their blue Ford station wagon and had two little windows decorated with frilly curtains—it was a home away from home, or at least a comfortable bedroom away from home.

The kids were still small, and we were on the first of what would be many camping trips with Harry and Pat and their family. Harry was a great outdoorsman who loved to camp, fish, and hunt, and he taught us a lot about camping. We had a ten-foot-by-sixteen-foot canvas tent, a sturdy cloth house really, but yes, I could see the advantages to a pop-up camper: no poles, no assembly, no leaks.

One time, we set up camp at the Hamlin Beach campground at Lake Ontario about forty miles from our homes for two whole weeks. Harry and I would commute daily to our workplaces at NTID, while Vicki and Pat and the children would go to the beach, to lay out in the sun, play in the water, and cook hot lunches on our Coleman stove.

Years later, on one of our best camping trips with the Scofields, we spent two weeks at one of the Thousand Islands near the Canadian border, using our large tent for both families. Harry took us in his boat to the island, which was like a paradise with all its nature with no one else around.

Not all trips were as terrific, though. One summer, we were camped at Sampson State Park between Seneca and Cayuga Lakes, two of the glacial Finger Lakes in the Southern Tier of New York state. The lakes are more than thirty miles long and over 400 feet deep at their deepest points. As soon as we erected our tent at the campsite, it began to rain so hard the roof and walls of the tent shuddered nonstop. We could feel the rumble of thunder as flashes of lightning illuminated the tent. Could lightning strike us through the canvas? Yes, of course, it could! We scrambled out of our sleeping bags and gathered them up into our arms before dashing out of the tent, through the torrential rain, and to the campsite bathrooms, where we slept, protected from the dirty concrete floors of the women's bathroom only by our sleeping bags.

At 5:00 the next morning, before the sun was entirely above the horizon, a park ranger entered the bathroom and said, "You folks have to clear out of here by six o'clock because other campers will be coming in to use the toilets and the sinks."

When we returned to our campsite, our sleeping bags hugged to our chests and our feet sinking in mud, we found our tent flattened and soaking wet, covered in small puddles. We decided to drive to nearby Ovid for a hearty breakfast at a diner. Afterward, we went back to the campsite to pack up everything except the tent, which we set up to dry. A few days later, I drove back about two hours to the campsite to take the tent down and bring it home.

"Let's get a pop-up camper!" I said to Vicki when I returned home with our tent. She was in full agreement, and so that same month we bought one, which we enjoyed frequently using over the next five years. Back then, it was easy to get ready for a camping weekend at the last minute, depending on the weather on a Thursday afternoon or Friday morning, and finding a spot. Unfortunately, a few years later, competition stiffened, and we had to reserve campsites far in advance—at least six months for popular sites. The problem was we never knew what the weather would be like during the times we reserved a site for—this was before the internet was readily available—and if we had to cancel plans because of rain or cold, then all four of us would be disappointed.

As our children grew, Bernard became more involved with Little League and other activities, Stephanie with summer camps. More and more often, our camper parked dormant in our backyard. By the time they were teenagers, and my job had become more demanding, we donated the camper to the Salvation Army. We'd loved every minute of the camping experiences. I must admit that I still miss those days, when we were in close quarters at night, with the starry sky outside the little windows, after a long day of hiking, swimming, or fishing together. We'd sit around the campfire, slapping bugs away, roasting marshmallows, and cooking over the fire. Sometimes we wouldn't see another family for hours or even days at a time—it was just the Hurwitzes out in nature, being together, soaking in the natural world.

INCREASINGLY, while technology and many other things have improved for deaf people over the years, travel has not. Even so, when I think back to some of our earlier cross-country odysseys, I marvel at how much has changed. One time we relied on the kindness of a train conductor at Grand Central Station to get a message to a fellow train conductor at Penn Station a few blocks away that we needed help making a connection to our Florida-bound train. We had missed the earlier connection since our train was late arriving in NYC from Rochester. We explained that we needed to catch up to our Florida-bound train because we had friends that were meeting us in Jacksonville and we had no way to contact them to tell them we'd missed our train. That first conductor personally put us in a cab headed to the other station and used his radio or phone to call and let the other conductor for the DC express train know to look for us. We made the express train to Washington, DC, where we got off and got on our original connecting train from New York City to Jacksonville that was on the slower track and arrived one hour later. Once we arrived in Jacksonville, we met up with Merle and Susan Reekers and their two sons Scott and David. Crisis barely averted! We then enjoyed traveling with them in their RV throughout Florida.

Or the time Vicki and I decided to travel across the country for six weeks during the summer of 1996. The trip would prove to be one of the sweet highlights of our marriage, but it was also marked by challenges caused by our reliance, as deaf people, on technology. Driving our minivan, we set off for Minnesota to visit with our friends. From there, we drove on through North Dakota. We had brought our Compact (a portable TTY) in a cushioned case, so we could maintain contact with our children, a laptop to keep up with our work emails, and a decoder to enjoy the benefits of closed-captioned TV programs in motels. After about a week on the road, we stopped in Cody, Wyoming, for the night. The next morning, we checked out of the motel, and I carried several bags to the car. We then headed for Yellowstone Park. After a harrowing all-day drive on winding roads, some snow-covered, through the mountains, we drove into Montana and stopped in Ennis to stay overnight in a hotel. Vicki and I unloaded the minivan quickly and carried all our things to the room. Vicki was anxious to use the TTY to call our children. But we couldn't find it among our things in the room. I went back to the minivan but couldn't find it there either.

Back in our room, I suddenly felt ill, like I'd swallowed a brick. I remembered putting the TTY on top of the minivan that morning after checking out of the motel in Wyoming! I could picture it on the van's roof. I ran back to the vehicle to see if it was still there. Of course, it wasn't, so I sheepishly admitted to Vicki what I had done.

I went to the motel office and asked the clerk to call the motel clerk in Cody, Wyoming, to see if someone had found the TTY. The staff went out to look for it and couldn't find it but promised to call back if they ever located it. Naturally, we were sick about what happened.

"Maybe we can use our laptop to send an email to our kids?" Vicki wondered. There was no other TTY in the entire town of Ennis, in the middle of nowhere in Montana. We hadn't felt so isolated in a long time. On top of it, we couldn't use our laptop even to read and send emails, since there was no internet connection. Thank heavens we had the TV decoder. I hooked it up to the old TV in the room, and we entertained ourselves with a good movie with captions.

The next morning, we stopped at a different motel elsewhere in Montana that had internet service to send email messages to our children to reassure them that we'd keep in touch via email until we could find a payphone with a TTY.

Three days later, we arrived in Portland for the NAD convention. Vicki and I entertained the idea of buying a new portable TTY, priced somewhere between $200 and $400, from one of the exhibitors, but we held off. The next day, I got an email from Bernard telling me that he had called his answering machine back home and found a message from a woman in Cody who had discovered our Compact TTY on the road between Cody and Yellowstone Park. She looked inside the case and saw our son's telephone number.

You can imagine how flabbergasted I was. I immediately called the woman through a relay service using a payphone TTY in the hotel lobby. She offered to send the Compact TTY, which didn't seem damaged, to me wherever I wanted. I asked if she'd send it by Federal Express to our hotel in Portland, and that we'd send her a check. The next day, we received the package with the Compact TTY inside, in perfect condition, despite its fall from the van and time on the road.

The rest of that trip included (but was not limited to) a visit with Bernard and his future wife Stacy for three nights in the San Francisco Bay area, and an overnight stay with our friends, Paul and Anne Ogden, in Fresno. We then traveled on to Yosemite, Death Valley National Park, and Barstow, California, where it was more than 100 degrees. The hot air was thick with the aroma of cow manure, and so we went on to Arizona, New Mexico, and the Grand Canyon. We arrived in St. Louis in time to attend a CID alumni reunion, after which we drove on to Omaha, Nebraska, for the American Society for Deaf Children conference, where Vicki and I gave a presentation for parents of deaf children. From there, we drove to my hometown of Sioux City and onward to Lake Okoboji, where we stayed for a week at a lake resort. We were on our way to Chicago when we saw a sign advertising the "Field of Dreams," the place in Dyersville, Iowa, where they filmed the movie of the same name. We drove to the ballpark, ringed by cornfields, sat on the bleachers, and reminisced about the movie. It was surreal and awesome to see.

By the time we made it back home to Rochester, our eyes full of this vast country's majesty, Vicki and I marveled that we'd managed to spend nearly every minute of the entire six weeks together, happier and more in harmony than ever. Most of the time on our trip, we talked and talked, but other times, we were quiet and reflected on what we experienced during our long drives through the beautiful country.

WHEN BERNARD BEGAN his first year at Princeton University, and Stephanie was in high school, Vicki was ready to work full-time. She applied at Substance and Alcohol Intervention Services for the Deaf in downtown Rochester. Although she didn't get the job, she was referred to work as a social worker at Norris Clinic. This residential alcoholism treatment center had a unit for deaf and hard of hearing clients with severe drug and alcohol addictions. Vicki was the only deaf employee and shared an office with Pat Morrison, who was both a social worker and interpreter. Although Vicki had an excellent supervisor, some hearing employees treated her as if she were an assistant, expecting her to provide a Deaf culture class for them. She told them that her job description did not include that responsibility and advised them to find someone from NTID. For sixteen months, Vicki provided her clients with individual, group, and family therapy and behavior modification.

About two years before Vicki started at the Norris Clinic, she'd applied for a position as a coordinator for student development in the student life team in the Department of Human Development at NTID and didn't get it. More than a year later, the department encouraged Vicki to apply again. They offered her a five-year position on the condition that she obtain a master's degree. Hence, she enrolled in the Careers and Human Resources Development (CHRD) graduate program at RIT. At the age of forty-nine, she graduated with a master's degree in CHRD—a year after Bernard graduated from Princeton and a year before Stephanie graduated from RSD. After five years' work with the student life team, she had to reapply for the same position, although this time it would be permanent. After a round of interviews and other candidates vying for the position, she got the job for another eight years.

As a part of Vicki's graduate studies, she developed a curriculum for a pilot course in Deaf women's studies, which she taught at NTID for ten years while working with the Department of Student Life. The course was the first of its kind in the country at the time, in 1993. Vicki loved her job and had wonderful colleagues. She also taught courses in freshmen seminar and Deaf heritage. After seventeen years of service, Vicki retired from NTID in 2001.

Once retired, she planned to return to being a homemaker now that her children had completed their college educations, and she looked forward to doing projects at home. This aspiration was short-lived, however, because Dr. Harold Mowl, RSD superintendent and CEO, approached her about applying for the open position as director of the RSD Outreach Center. She was hesitant since she wanted to retire, but decided to give it a chance. Years earlier, she had wanted to work in a school setting where she could provide resources to deaf children and especially their families. Here was her chance. She took the job and went on to have a very successful career at RSD. She was instrumental in developing a variety of outreach services for students and their families in other schools in the area ranging from Lake Ontario to the Southern Tier and from Batavia to near Syracuse. She oversaw sign language classes for parents, the Rochester After-School Academy, and the Sign Communication Proficiency Interview.

Additionally, along with the Monroe County Intervention Services and Marty Talbot of the Boards of Cooperative Educational Services, Vicki developed, published, and widely distributed a comprehensive resource manual on services for families of children with hearing loss. After work, she continued teaching Deaf women's studies as an adjunct faculty at NTID. After four years at RSD, she retired for the final time.

Vicki continued to be involved in the Deaf community after founding several organizations for deaf women and receiving numerous awards. She was the cofounder of Deaf Women of Rochester and Advocacy Services for Abused Deaf Victims in Rochester, now known as IGNITE. She served as vice president on the national board of Deaf Women United and was the editor for the *ESNews,* a publication organ of the ESAD in New York. She also served as the editor of the CID alumni association newsletter.

As a student at RSD, Stefi was in a class of eight students in their senior year. It so happened that seven of them wanted to go to Gallaudet, even though NTID was also a good choice. But having lived in Rochester most of their lives, they wanted to go to a college away from home.

"I'm worried Gallaudet might not be a good fit for her," Vicki said to me one day.

"It would be a challenge, true," I said. Despite Stefi's academic, emotional, and social challenges at RSD, we nevertheless supported her decision to go to Gallaudet with the hope that she'd receive strong support from her teachers and counselors. Most of her RSD classmates were admitted as regular freshman students, while Stefi and two others were placed in the Prep Year program at the Northwest Campus eight miles from Gallaudet's main campus.

"This will be good!" Vicki said. We were thrilled Stefi would be in the smaller group, able to focus on her academic, social, and emotional needs. Over time, our hopes proved well-founded. The prep program allowed her to get into a comprehensive evaluation program that addressed her past struggles in school. Stefi had excellent teachers and counselors who helped her with her ADHD issues. And her par-

Stefi.

ticipation in the varsity softball team on the main campus at Gallaudet gave her an outstanding balance between the academic, physical,
and social aspects of college life.

Interestingly, after one year at Gallaudet, all of Stefi's six classmates from RSD withdrew—some leaving college altogether, others
transferring to other colleges. Stefi remained as the sole RSD student
in her class during the second year. Since Gallaudet decided to close
down the Northwest Campus and move all the prep students to the
main campus, Stefi spent her second year on the main campus, which
she loved. She continued to play on the varsity softball team. Still,
the academic side of college continued to be a struggle for her, so she
decided to transfer to NTID in her junior year, which we believed was
another excellent decision for her. Although she continued to have
struggles in academics, she loved being back home at NTID and happily participated in campus activities, including a sorority. She had an
excellent counselor by the name of Lee Twyman, who gave her excellent emotional support as her academic and social advisor. At NTID,
she completed her associate degree requirements in applied computer

technology. As an alumna of both NTID and Gallaudet, she is fortunate to have friends with people from both colleges and continues to associate with them in the community. To this day, she loves camping with her friends.

Bernard graduated from Princeton in 1992 with a major in politics, a minor in history, and a secondary school teaching certificate. He student-taught at a Catholic all-girls school and did an internship one summer with Congresswoman Louise Slaughter's office in Washington, DC. After graduation from college, Bernard went to Poland to teach English and spent several months traveling in Poland and Eastern Europe, where he took the opportunity to learn more about our family history. He then worked as a legislative assistant for New York Senator Mary Ellen Jones for a couple of years before attending the University of Buffalo School of Law, where he specialized in education law. He also did a year as a visiting student at Cornell Law School, studying labor and employment law.

NOT FAR FROM the camping sites where we'd parked our pop-up camper in our family camping heyday stands the beautiful Belhurst Castle, on the shores of Seneca Lake near Geneva, NY. The morning of Bernard's wedding day, the rain poured down steadily, and Vicki and I glanced nervously out the window of our room, praying the rain would stop. The plan was for Bernard to marry his love, Stacy Lawrence, outside on the lawn at four o'clock.

As I tied my tie in the mirror, I winced at the unsightly bandage over my forehead. The day before, I'd stepped out of my shower, rushing to get ready for the rehearsal dinner, and I slipped and fell. When I shot my arm out, trying to grab one of the towel bars, it broke off the wall. My head hit the edge of the bathroom counter. The big gash on my forehead bled profusely, and Stefi rushed me to the ER, where they gave me stitches and covered the wound.

Little did I know that on the morning of the wedding, Stacy's father was suffering a similar mishap. He stood up quickly after picking up something he'd dropped on the bathroom floor and bashed his forehead against the sink counter, also breaking open the skin on his forehead.

Bernard graduating from Princeton after signing I-LOVE-YOU to us on his way to the stage.

Miraculously, it stopped raining around noon and was sunny all afternoon. Since Stacy is Catholic, they decided to have both a rabbi and a priest officiate the wedding as a team. Father Tom Coughlin and Rabbi Alan Abarbanell led the beautiful ceremony in ASL. Sun glinted off the wet grass, Bernard and Stacy stood beneath the chuppah, and tears flowed down many faces. It was perfect, and everyone loved it.

After the ceremony, we all went inside (Stacy's father and I identically bandaged) to the ballroom for a reception and dinner, and the rain started up again, big sheets of water pouring down, with thunder and lightning. Rain on a wedding day, a blessing for everyone, especially the bride and the groom.

Bernard was a practicing attorney for two private firms, Harter Secrest & Emery and Nixon Peabody, for a total of four years and then worked as an editor for three years at the publisher Thomson West (now Thomson Reuters), which publishes law books. He then served for five years as a labor relations attorney for a local board of cooperative educational services that oversaw twenty-two school districts. He worked closely with superintendents, school boards, and unions and is currently associate vice president of RIT for the Office of NTID Administration, a role he has had since 2011.

Bernard and Stacy, who is deaf, now have two adorable children, both hearing. Susan Juliette is a fourth-year student at Hobart and William Smith Colleges in Geneva, New York, where she was recruited as a coxswain of the varsity women's rowing team and later selected as team captain in her second year. She completed her study abroad in Ecuador and Ireland. Ethan is a high school senior and a budding baseball star who plays third base, my old position, and pitches. He also plays other infield positions. Pretty soon, he will be deciding where to go to college. Of course, Vicki and I are grandparents bursting with pride about their accomplishments.

17

My First 100 Days at Gallaudet

As VICKI AND I HID offstage behind the curtain, the board chair stood at the podium and thanked the search committee for its excellent work. He then turned to look at us—from his place on stage, he could see us standing in the wings, wearing the Gallaudet ball caps and jackets we'd been given for the occasion and asked both Vicki and me to come to the stage. We stepped out from behind the curtain and walked onto the large stage. To our amazement, the crowd was huge—nearly a thousand people standing and waving their arms in celebration. They hadn't known until this moment who the board had selected as their university's next president, and they seemed to be happy it was me. How heartwarming! I pointed to Vicki and said, "Here's the First Lady," and walked the rest of the way across the stage, up to the podium. My hands were shaking, and there was nothing I could do about it. Luckily, I had my notes with me. I'm not sure I could have spoken off the cuff. My hands continued to tremble a bit as I signed my prepared speech.

My speech was not interrupted by protesters like those who had protested in 2006 when the Gallaudet board selected an internal presidential candidate. Vicki and I were both relieved. After my brief speech, we were hurriedly escorted through the auditorium and lobby as people reached out to greet and congratulate us. Handlers rushed us to a private room for an interview with the *Washington Post*. As I was answering the reporter's questions, I felt impatient to be free again to talk with the well-wishers in the lobby. The presidential transition team, the board chair, and the vice chair were in the room with the reporter and us.

"Did you sympathize with the students who protested the board's selection of an inside candidate in 2006?" the reporter asked me.

I didn't feel right answering one way or the other, but as I was wondering what in the world I should say, Vice Chair Frank Wu, bless him, quickly took over. "That's not a fair question to ask someone who wasn't here and wasn't involved. And it's especially not a fair question to ask a brand-new president!"

We'd been in the small room with the reporter for upward of an hour by now. To our disappointment, when we finally emerged, only a few people remained in the lobby. Most had already left since it was a Sunday, and they wanted to go home to be with their families. Later, I was quick to advise the board never to allow this to happen to future president-designates. They should first be allowed to mingle with the community before being interviewed by reporters.

Vicki and I—still dazed—strolled around the city that afternoon and had a leisurely dinner in the evening. We flew back home to Rochester the next morning.

My next challenge was to help President Destler find someone to become the interim president of NTID. We had only two-and-a-half months before we would move to Washington, DC, to start my new position as the president of Gallaudet University on January 1, 2010. I recommended Jim DeCaro for the interim president position, and Dr. Destler agreed and asked me to approach Jim about it.

At first, to my dismay, Jim declined. He was not happy about my leaving for Gallaudet and wanted me to stay during his tenure with PEN-International. After a few days, I asked Jim and his wife, Pat, to join Vicki and me at our favorite ice cream store at Schoen's Place on the Erie Canal. Though we had a good chat, Jim was unwavering about not assuming the interim presidency. I was disappointed. But the next morning, Jim emailed to let me know he thought it over and agreed to accept my invitation. That was a great relief for me!

I informed President Destler of Jim's willingness to serve in my absence, which allowed me to focus on wrapping up my responsibilities and preparing for our move. Though we agreed that Jim would begin on December 1, I would remain until the end of December during the transition.

"Don," I said, "I would love it if you came to Gallaudet with me to be my chief of staff."

"Thanks," Don said to me with a sad smile, shaking his head. "But as soon as you leave, I plan to retire and move to California to be with Marian and our kids' families."

Don Beil, my executive assistant at NTID, had been maintaining a long-distance marriage ever since Marian had moved to the Bay Area a couple of years earlier to be close to their sons and grandchildren.

"I understand," I said. I couldn't help myself but add: "Please just consider my offer. Remember how much you loved living in Washington, DC, with Marian thirty years ago? And it's only gotten better. I think we can do big things at Gallaudet, and I think you'd enjoy being part of that."

"OK," he said. "I'll think it over."

After some mulling, Don did agree to work with me for no more than six months to allow me to get started and settled. I told him it would be a good arrangement because I wanted him to join my staff, even if only for a short time. Knowing that Don planned to stay only six months, I agreed to allow him to fly home to California to be with his family for one week each month while he worked at Gallaudet.

In October 2009, I sent out a memo to the Gallaudet community to offer my warm greetings and to announce Don Beil as my new chief of staff. I also included the itinerary for my weeklong campus visit and looked forward to meeting as many people as possible during our stay. In November, Vicki and I flew to Washington for a week so I could meet with the vice presidents, the provost, the deans, and the executive directors, as well as my chief of staff and the office managers who would report to me as direct reports, and become more acclimated to the campus environment.

Our new home was to be House One, the on-campus, fully furnished presidential residence, also known as the Edward Miner Gallaudet Residence or President's House, a thirty-five-room Victorian Gothic mansion designed by Vaux, Withers & Co. in 1867. Because it would be our home only for the duration of my service as president, we wondered what to do with our house in Pittsford, NY. Sell it? Rent it out? Keep it and find a way to have someone watch the house for us? We thought of our daughter, Stefi, who was working part-time at Family Services Foundation in Frederick, Maryland; she had thought about moving back to Rochester. Stefi hadn't had any luck finding a full-time permanent job with full benefits. With that in mind, we asked her if she'd want to move into and take care of our house while we were in Washington, DC. Though she was at first thrilled with the idea, she then realized the irony: Stefi had looked forward to us being closer to her while she was in Maryland! Even so, she moved into our house in December 2009 and immediately landed a great job as a day and residential habilitation staff member at the Center for Disability Rights. In the fall of 2010, she became a teaching assistant for preschool children at RSD.

Debbie DeStefano, who worked in the president's office as a liaison to the Gallaudet University Board of Trustees, was already waiting for us at the entrance kiosk. After we greeted each other, she led us to the Campus Safety Office at Carlin Hall. We registered for our ID cards, had photos taken, and picked up keys to House 400 on the MSSD Hill, our temporary housing for one month while House One was cleaned, painted, and repaired.

The following Monday, January 4, I walked from House 400 to my new office in College Hall.

"Good morning, President Hurwitz!" Don Beil said when I walked in. He'd beaten me to the office and was ready to work. Over those first few days, I met with each of my direct reports and with the representatives of the student body government, faculty senate, and staff council. I met with Debbie DeStefano and Paul Blakely, both of whom were extremely helpful in getting me started. Daun Banks was the first administrative assistant I had in the office. Pat Thompson, who earlier retired from Gallaudet but returned as a temporary secretary, was very helpful, too.

At that time, Paul Blakely was working 40 percent of his time in the Office of the President and the other 60 percent as an assistant to Dean of Student Affairs Dwight Benedict. Approximately three months later, at my request, Dwight and I agreed to increase Paul's time allocation to 65 percent with the Office of the President. Over time, Paul's position with the Office of the President became a full-time position, and he took over the responsibilities as the manager for the Office of the President and House One. All staff employees within the Office of the President reported to him.

While Don, my chief of staff, was more of a visionary person, he worked closely with the board, vice presidents, deans, and directors to implement action plans set forth by the board and the president. Don prepared annual reports to the US Department of Education and coordinated congressional visits for me.

When Vicki met Paul during the November visit, they easily and quickly clicked, especially since both were Virginia natives. Paul and Vicki, "partners in crime" as they called each other, worked together to get House One ready for our move-in on February 2. They had some wallpaper stripped off, repainted walls, and rearranged furniture on the second and third floors—everything was done to freshen and maintain, and also to make sure Vicki and I could feel at home. It is a huge place, five or six times the size of any house we'd ever lived in before, with three floors of living space, a full basement, and a small attic under a cupola. We occupied the second and third floors; our master bedroom and my office were on the second floor, and the family room, small kitchen, and Vicki's office were on the third floor. The large kitchen on the first floor was used primarily by the catering service for special university events. One of the rooms in the basement was my exercise room. Although it also had a sauna and a cedar closet for bottles of wine, we didn't use them.

Shortly after our move into House One, people frequently asked whether we saw ghosts. Vicki's response from that day on to today has been, "Yes, there are ghosts, but I didn't see them." The first night after dinner in the upstairs small kitchen, I started my usual routine of washing dishes. I noticed there was no hot water and asked Vicki, who was puzzled because she had hot water while she cooked. We contacted Paul, who then contacted a plumber. He came right away and checked—no hot water. But there was hot water in the bathroom on the same floor! Puzzled, he went to the basement to check and came back up. Still no hot water. He went back down and tried to fix it. Yes, hot water came back on. The next morning, there was no hot water . . . again . . . so Paul was contacted again, and the plumber came back. There was hot water.

Was that a ghost playing tricks on us? There were many different incidents with Casper, our friendly ghost, and after the second year, the tricks stopped. Maybe because he figured we're fit to live in the house after all. Who knows?

In 2011, we commissioned Sander Blondeel, a deaf Belgian artist, to create a substantial stained glass piece to cover the unsightly view of the gas station from one of the windows in Vicki's office. The stained glass depicted butterflies, College Hall, and House One. The Capitol also could be viewed from the other window in Vicki's office. We later donated this piece to Gallaudet University; it is now on display in the ASL and Deaf Studies Department in the Sorenson Language and Communication Center.

Paul and his staff immediately worked on a plan for my inauguration as the tenth president of Gallaudet University. It took place on Wednesday, May 12, which coincidentally was my father's birthday, and on the same week as Gallaudet's commencement. Our families and friends from all over the country were in attendance.

While the board of trustees had been contemplating who to select from the four presidential finalists, twenty-six members and friends of the Washington Society of the Jewish Deaf were touring in Israel. By chance, all four of us finalists were Jewish, so the group decided to buy a mezuzah in Israel for the front door of House One and present it to whoever was selected. As soon as they learned that I was the president-designate, they contacted me about setting up a mezuzah blessing ceremony. Rabbi Darby Leigh, the deaf son of Irene Leigh and David Leigh, whom we'd known since before Darby was born, officiated the ceremony. Afterward, Vicki and I added other mezuzahs to four other doors on the first floor.

"HAPPY SO FAR?" I asked Vicki at our breakfast table one morning, the early winter sun slanting in from outside. We were both dressed for the day, and I had already done my daily exercise on my stationary bike.

"Yes!" she said, "very happy, but worried about you. I'm worried this job might put a lot of stress on you!"

"Don't worry," I said. "I've got lots of energy, and I'm excited about doing the work. What about you? Do you think you'll have enough to do as First Lady?"

Knowing her as I did, I knew that she would soon be as busy as I was. And I was right. Vicki was a natural at all the things that would make her a beloved First Lady of Gallaudet University: mistress of ceremonies, teacher, hostess of receptions, and a good friend to people all across the campus, from students to professors and members of the administration. Vicki quickly embraced her role and delved into voluntary services for the university. She served as a guest presenter for social work and freshman seminar courses and at events. Vicki often visited the students in the Deaf women's studies class. And she especially enjoyed hosting receptions at House One.

"When I retire," I teased her, "they are not going to let you leave."

"Because I didn't apply for this job and don't have a contract or a job description," she told me, "I just get to do what I enjoy doing!"

Many alumni remarked that Vicki was very much like the beloved Frances Merrill, the wife of Gallaudet President Edward "Pete" Merrill, during his presidency from 1969 to 1983. And whenever Vicki and I went on the road, we had fun presenting together about Gallaudet University. I'd talk about the mission of the university and the goals and activities that were established and accomplished, and Vicki would speak about the history of House One and the First Ladies of Gallaudet. People were often surprised to learn that she was not the first nor the second, but the third deaf First Lady. Vicki always explained that the first one was Ethel Zoe Taylor Hall, who married Professor Percival Hall following her graduation from Gallaudet. Dr. Hall subsequently served as the second president of Gallaudet University. The second was Donna Davila, spouse of Dr. Robert R. Davila, the ninth president of Gallaudet.

Being installed as president of Gallaudet with my grandchildren in attendance.

Vicki appreciated the rich history of House One and was surprised that many alumni had never set foot in it. With the help of Gerri Frank, who retired in 1997 as the administrative assistant to five Gallaudet presidents, and Mike Olson in the Gallaudet Archives, Vicki researched its history. Video producer Lizzie Sorkin and digital video technician Suzanne Scheuermann, along with staff from the Technology and Video Services Department, developed a DVD about the history of House One that Vicki narrated. It was widely distributed and used as a fundraiser for the establishment of the Gallaudet Museum (now known as the National Deaf Life Museum) led by Dr. Jane Norman, director emeritus, with Vicki as the honorary chair of the Friends of the Museum.

DURING OUR FIRST SUMMER in Washington, we were faced with unwelcome visitors picnicking on warm evenings on the private front lawn of House One. And frequently, some hearing, non-Gallaudet folks from off-campus would walk right up to the house to peer into the windows, which never failed to frighten or startle Vicki. As a result, the Facilities Department built a fence from the Seventh Street gateway up to the driveway just before the front side of the house while we were out of town. When we returned and saw the eight-foot-high fence, we were horrified at its height. Facilities eventually replaced it with another fence that was only about four feet high. We were disappointed and hurt when some members of the Gallaudet community expressed concern and suspicion regarding our new fence: Where did the funds for this fence come from, they asked? We felt that it was a necessary improvement. Fortunately, after people saw how nice it looked and how it enhanced House One's overall role as a symbol of the university and a real residence all in one, the questions faded away. Having the fence was especially helpful when Vicki hosted kindergarteners and first, second, and third graders to garden with her at House One because they were able to play games and run around freely and safely on the front lawn.

AT RIT/NTID, I had enjoyed having a full-time designated interpreter who accompanied me on all my travels and to most of my meetings. At Gallaudet, I worked with the Gallaudet Interpreting Services to identify a small group of interpreters who could work with me as designated interpreters. Unlike RIT, which is a mainstreamed campus, almost everyone at Gallaudet was fluent in ASL and rarely used interpreters in staff meetings. Some interpreters might show up to aid a no-taker in selected cabinet meetings by voicing for those who use ASL without their voice. At Gallaudet, I was fortunate to have a cadre of highly skilled interpreters with whom I could easily fit in many meetings off-campus, such as congressional meetings, community board meetings, and meetings with donors, trustees, and nonsigning campus visitors.

AFTER THE Middle States Commission in Higher Education (MSCHE) placed the university on probation in 2006 due to its unsatisfactory response to the MSCHE's fourteen requirements, Dr. Robert Davila stepped in as the interim president on January 1, 2007. He immediately assigned his senior administrators and key faculty and staff members to develop responses to each of the MSCHE's fourteen requirements. The university ultimately received a positive response from MSCHE, with a status change from probation to warning and finally to satisfactory within seven months.

Then the board of trustees decided to commission a five-year strategic plan to address the remaining shortcomings and guide the university's future work, laying out benchmarks and clear goals with the help of an external consultant, Booz Allen Hamilton. During the presidential search process, I'd been handed a packet about this newly adopted Gallaudet Strategic Plan (GSP), which had already been approved by the board of trustees in the summer of 2009. At first, it seemed like a favorable position for me to be in—serving as a new president who already had a clear set of instructions.

But the GSP's existence would prove to be a challenge. When I arrived on the campus in January 2010, leaders of the faculty senate explained to me that the previous administration had not sufficiently consulted the faculty during the plan's creation. They also outlined how the shared governance principles the university was supposed to follow had not been fully incorporated as well. The definition of the bilingual philosophy on campus was a significant point of contention. Several faculty leaders believed that it should refer solely to proficiency in both ASL and written English. In contrast, some trustees felt that the English component should have been in a broader context that included spoken English. The faculty was also concerned that the GSP was too detailed and contained too many subcomponents under each of the five strategic goals: enrollment, retention, revenue generation, academic quality, and research.

I began to see that I was at a disadvantage—too late to the scene. I hadn't had the privilege of initiating a new strategic planning process with the Gallaudet community. Not only was it a plan developed before I'd arrived, but I also was left with a board mandate to implement the GSP at the earliest possible time.

"My first 100 days are going to be key," I told Vicki one night over dinner in Rochester, before we moved to Washington. So crucial, in fact, that I had drafted an ambitious and comprehensive plan for what I wanted to put into place in my first few months at Gallaudet and how I was going to enlist the work and expertise of the people around me to make it work.

When I presented my 100-Day Plan to the board a month before my start date, I stressed to them that my focus as president would be on *people*. People make things work or fail. People are the source of all ideas. People, and their positive relationships with each other, had always been the cause of any success I'd ever had. I asked the board to consider the categories in my plan to show that my priority was to work with people on campus to implement the GSP. The board subsequently endorsed the proposed 100-Day Plan. I also shared principles for expectations and essential qualities for a successful cabinet, which enabled me to proceed with my entering the presidency.

It was my intention during the first 100 days and throughout my presidency to be as visible and available as possible, particularly for students. I expressed my desire for the community at Gallaudet to gain an understanding of my expectations throughout the university. My transparency, ability to communicate clearly, and especially my ability to encourage people smarter than myself to do great work, had served me well in Rochester. And the leaders I had most enjoyed working for had been those whose goals and standards were clear and understandable. These early days were a time for people to become comfortable with me and confident in my ability to build personal relationships of trust with others. I wanted the community to have renewed confidence in Gallaudet and a sense of teamwork for the good of our students and the university.

After I'd shared the 100-Day Plan with the cabinet, I assigned cabinet officers to implement the goals related to their respective roles and responsibilities. We developed a long list of proposed agenda items for discussion with the cabinet over the next four to six months. One of the highest priorities was to establish task forces to assess and prioritize academic programs, student services, and administrative services that would enable the university to make sound decisions on using its financial resources to support the university's needs on a priority basis.

The 100-Day Plan provided us with a road map for between four and six months (accounting for weekends and holidays). It had seven categories: composition and duties of the Gallaudet president's cabinet; GSP implementation; governance groups; the board of trustees; my office's relationship with students, staff, and faculty; external af-

My cabinet at Gallaudet University.

fairs (in particular the relationships among the university and various government regulatory and funding agencies); and finally, other mandatory work, like travel and campus events that were already planned or would need to be.

I established the new cabinet as a new leadership team. The purpose was to expand membership that would ensure a broader and more diverse representation of the Gallaudet community. The cabinet's charge was to carry out the university's mission.

I emphasized that although most cabinet members would continue their current reporting relationships, over time, I expected changes to occur in the president's office. Membership on the cabinet might expand or contract over time as a reflection of changing needs.

"I want you all to represent the broadest of university perspectives," I explained at our first meeting, "not just your current areas of assignments." By using a team approach, my cabinet would work toward consensus in the best interests of the university and students, rather than advocating for their respective areas.

The Gallaudet Board of Trustees during my administration.

I explained that other individuals might be invited to participate in certain meetings, or parts of such meetings, depending on the agenda, which may benefit from their input, insights, and feedback.

My 100-Day Plan item regarding the GSP clarified that key senior administrators would implement the strategic plan by involving faculty, staff, students, and specific external individuals to develop action plans for attaining each objective.

I wanted to build a sense of the importance of various governance groups to the success of the university by meeting with those groups. These meetings were crucial for attending to their concerns, emphasizing how their participation enhanced the university and how we needed their help with addressing issues related to the GSP's implementation.

I assured the board that I would make all board activities as a high priority, ensure board needs were met, and provide regular communication. I indicated that I would collaborate with the board to formulate the president's plans of work and develop a new evaluation system to be reviewed and approved by the board at the April 2010 board meeting.

I also laid out a plan to take the necessary time to meet with and know people on campus through a wide variety of activities, ranging from simply walking around the school, to attending student and sports activities on campus, to hosting events for students, faculty, and staff at House One. I informed the board that I created a new chief of staff position in the Office of the President and that Don Beil from NTID was appointed to serve in this capacity.

Recognizing the need to build better public relations and improve marketing and development efforts at the university, I laid out a specific plan to work closely with leaders in these areas.

I would form a new university council made up of leaders from four governance groups—the faculty senate, the staff council, the student body government, and the graduate student council—along with key leaders from the cabinet. Bringing these people together in a forum would allow everyone to share each other's goals, activities, and accomplishments and also to discuss critical issues, needs, and concerns affecting the welfare of the university and students. The university council would keep the community posted on major issues that affected the university, such as the federal budget, academic affairs, student affairs, the facilities, and policies. The university council would be open to any member of the public who was interested in attending as an observer.

Regarding external relations, I presented a plan to fast-track meetings with key individuals on Capitol Hill, the US Department of Education and other federal agencies, national professional and consumer advocacy organizations, and major donors. I also reported that I would be traveling throughout the country over the next several months to meet with alumni chapters and solicit their support for the university.

The Alabama School for the Deaf and Blind and the Texas School for the Deaf invited me to give graduation speeches. I also committed to attend and participate in national conferences, including those for the NAD, the Conference of Educational Administrators Serving the Deaf, and the International Congress on Education of the Deaf.

I outlined how the president's office and I would work with Vicki, as the university's First Lady, to organize receptions for students, faculty, alumni, donors, congressional representatives, and other visitors to House One. And lastly, the university's 150th anniversary celebration was only four years away and would have to be appropriately commemorated with marketing and events.

As a part of the charge to the community related to the GSP's implementation, I formed two major task forces to allow a complete assessment of the university's strategic plan and operations. One task force focused on academic programs and the other on administrative programs and services. The main reason for these two task forces was to demonstrate to the campus community that to run a university successfully, a president must get feedback from as many stakeholders as possible. It was an opportunity for the university to conduct a comprehensive review of its existing programs and services.

Upon receiving final reports from both task forces and in consultation with the board, I assigned the recommendations to senior administrators—vice presidents, the provost, and deans—to review and implement the recommended action plans. (Most completed them in a timely fashion over the next few years.) These implemented strategies were helpful in the university's self-review in time for the university's next full assessment by the MSCHE in 2012 and 2013.

I was impressed with the intense work of the task force committees. I felt that interested individuals in the Gallaudet community had sufficient occasions for dialogue with the administration before decisions were made related to university budget priorities and resource allocations aligned with the GSP. Although some community members expressed concern or disagreed with a few decisions, the rationale for each choice was made clear to the community. The university must be able to reallocate its finite resources to the high-priority areas, those focused on students and the university as a whole.

At the end of January, my first month at Gallaudet, it was a balmy sixty-eight degrees in Washington. Vicki and I joked that our friends back in Rochester were probably still hidden in layers of puffy coats and hats. But then, a few days later, on February 5, it snowed over seventeen inches in twenty-four hours, blanketing the campus and the entire city. "Snowmageddon," the biggest snowstorm in decades, was all anyone could talk about. We canceled classes. A few well-prepared students and faculty glided across campus on cross-country skis while other students built massive snowmen in the quads. And then a week later, it snowed another ten inches. Vicki and I enjoyed the winter wonderland view from our kitchen window.

My first 100 days were not without their expected share of controversy. That spring, the Gallaudet Department of Art, Communication, and Theatre chose *Corpus Christi*, a satirical play, for its spring production. Written by Terrence McNally in 1997, the play dramatizes the story of Jesus and the Apostles, depicting them as gay men living in modern-day Texas. Judas betrays Jesus because of sexual jealousy, and Jesus administers gay marriage between two apostles. Unsurprisingly, some people found the idea of the play blasphemous. A group of Gallaudet students—along with fundamentalist Christians not a part of the Gallaudet community —objected to the play and demanded its cancellation. "Just as everyone is entitled to their own good reputation," a protest organizer wrote online, "Gallaudet University has no right to harm and slander the spotless reputation of the God-Man with blasphemy, then run to academic freedom for cover."

For several days, my office's phone lines lit up with calls from protesters. Tarleton State University in Texas had just canceled a production of the same play as a result of similar pressure and even threats of violence, fanned by a national organization called the Defense of Tradition, Family, and Property. Dr. Steve Weiner, the provost, and I decided it would be best to open up a dialogue with the concerned students and see if we could arrive at a consensus. The students were not

I. King Jordan, myself, and Robert Davila at the twenty-fifth anniversary celebration of Deaf President Now.

satisfied and contacted external religious groups to become involved. I received over 30,000 emails and letters by snail mail.

The mounting pressure did not shake our confidence in some basic principles: freedom of expression, the role of art, and Gallaudet's responsibility to both as a leading liberal arts university. Provost Weiner issued a statement to *Inside Higher Ed*, which was covering the story, that encapsulated these principles beautifully: "Gallaudet University neither endorses nor condemns the views expressed in *Corpus Christi* or any dramatic production. We understand that there are people who will find this play affirming, liberating, and cathartic, and others who find its message disrespectful, distasteful, and repugnant. We seek to allow all views to be aired openly and respectfully, and we hope that open discussions will allow individuals to listen to one another. This is the hallmark of an academic institution."

The provost and I continued to work with both the theatre department chair and the director of the play to be sure there would be open pre- and postdialogues about the play. We wanted students to have the opportunity to gain a better appreciation for freedom of speech and expression.

When the play was performed, Vicki and I attended the opening night. Campus Safety officers and the DC Metropolitan Police Department were at the ready to ensure that the campus was safe for everyone (we had received threats of violence), including concerned playgoers. Protesters held signs and voiced their objections behind a rope that sectioned off an area for them. The series of open dialogues held before and after the play went smoothly, and it was a learning experience for all of us. I was particularly struck by statements from gay people about how hurtful it was to face a culture so antagonistic to a fundamental part of your self—who you want to be with, who you love. I also gained an understanding of the other perspective, of a devout believer who saw the theatrical exploration of Jesus's life as disrespectful and hurtful.

"It was very well performed," Vicki noted on the way home, and I agreed.

"The question-and-answer session afterward was very well handled too," I added.

The university administration and I believed that we had achieved the goal of fostering a climate of respect and understanding.

AT THE START of my presidency, I was pressed with a mandate by the board to reduce operating costs. One of the first things I did was implement internal cost controls, which helped reduce unnecessary expenditures, such as travel costs, consultant fees, and energy costs. We also implemented approval processes at different levels from managers and department chairs to deans and executive directors and finally to each respective vice president. This process helped to monitor expenditures and reduce costs wherever appropriate without compromising the quality of education and services for students.

Unfortunately, my administration anticipated that the federal appropriation would either be frozen or reduced over the next few years and the university's projected operational costs would continue to rise. I was faced with the immediate need to reduce staffing within the first four months of my presidency. The vice presidents, deans, executive directors, and department heads did their best to encourage employees who were laid off to apply for open essential positions. We also provided separation packages that included severance pay and professional assistance for seeking a new job or obtaining training. Although it was a painful and challenging process, my staff and I worked with human resources to ensure that the layoffs for each individual would be done as humanely and fairly as possible.

I have often wondered if I could have done things differently. Of course, I wish taking on such difficult decisions could have waited until I had at least a full year of the presidency under my belt. I was grateful to the vice presidents, deans, and executive directors for their willingness to work together to achieve the mandated reduction in force, as unpleasant as it was for all involved. Though difficult, the personnel reduction helped the university get into better financial shape, allowing the university to survive a 5.23 percent (or $6.1 million) cut to Gallaudet's federal appropriation.

Fortunately, after six months of operating without the $6.1 million in 2013, Congress temporarily restored the funds for the following fiscal year. We were still unsure whether the sequestration would be extended for the next ten years per law. Also, during my presidency, Gallaudet saw a significant increase in its endowment fund from $150 million in 2010 to close to $190 million in 2015. This helped support student needs and ensured the university's viability and sustainability.

The primary challenge for both Gallaudet University and RIT/NTID is recruiting students. Since the early 1970s, several federal laws—the Individuals with Disabilities Education Act (IDEA), Section 504 of the Rehabilitation Act, the Americans with Disabilities Act (ADA), and other civil rights laws—have made it possible for hearing colleges and universities to make their programs accessible, giving deaf students a more extensive choice of postsecondary programs they can attend.

Funding for a college education is another challenge among deaf or hard of hearing students because of a major reduction in vocational rehabilitation (VR) funds for students with disabilities who aspire to go to college. Many VR agencies, which are at the state level, keep students within their home states and often require them to attend a community college for at least two years before they transfer to Gallaudet or RIT/NTID.

Most college and universities have a student transfer rate of somewhere between 3 and 4 percent; for Gallaudet and RIT/NTID, the average is 25 to 30 percent. When speaking with other university presidents, I would explain that most transfer students who came to our colleges shared that they were searching for better opportunities to become fully engaged in college life.

Although deaf and hard of hearing students have more choices than in the past, "mainstreamed" colleges and universities can deprive deaf students of a meaningful college life experience. Where other than Gallaudet or RIT/NTID can deaf students become fully engaged in campus activities? Where else can a deaf student become president of the student body government, editor of the school newspaper, or land a leading role in theatrical productions? Where else can a deaf student-athlete become the captain of a sports team? I often shared with students and their families that a college education might take only four or five years, but could be some of the best times of their lives where they would form lifelong relationships with their peers. I also

Senator Harkin (front row, to the left of me) came to the ground breaking of the new MSSD dorm's site.

added that these experiences could lead to good jobs, enable them to become leaders, and create a good quality of life in their communities.

WE WERE FORTUNATE to have a truly wonderful friend in Senator Tom Harkin of Iowa (coincidently, Senator Harkin's deaf brother and my father were schoolmates at the Iowa School for the Deaf). He made sure that Gallaudet remained funded with a modest increase in the budget, while many other federal programs were either cut or eliminated. During my six years as president, Senator Harkin was also extremely helpful in securing funding of at least $7 million per year for the construction of a new MSSD dormitory, which amounted to $28 million over four years. Though he was unable to obtain the entire amount in a one-year federal appropriation, my staff and staff members in Senator Harkin's office worked out an extended appropriation plan that would spread the entire amount over the next several years. The new MSSD dormitory was completed and opened for student residents in January 2017.

18

Big Ideas

The board of trustees challenged me to come up with "big ideas" that would enable the university to move forward with its mission. Based on my dialogue with the cabinet and academic leaders, we determined that there was a great need to train and prepare deaf and hard of hearing individuals for careers in medicine and health care, law, business, and architecture. Hence, I proposed to the board that the university develop preprofessional programs in these four career areas. I explained that these preprofessional programs would encourage prospective students to consider Gallaudet as a first-choice four-year liberal arts university and realize that Gallaudet had a strong career focus. I further stated that it would also enable them to pursue their graduate studies in medicine and health care, law, business, and architecture in graduate schools. I was pleased that the board enthusiastically supported the proposal.

Gallaudet has long been recognized as a respected liberal arts university that prepares students for careers in psychology, social work, sociology, linguistics, ASL and Deaf studies, and other social science and humanities fields. That would continue; the preprofessional programs simply expanded the horizon of program offerings for young aspiring students who wanted the Gallaudet experience while coenrolling in one of the highly reputable universities in Washington, DC, to crossregister in coursework in their field of choice. Gallaudet had already been and continues to be one of the charter members of the

Consortium of Universities of the Washington Metropolitan Area, so it was an opportunity to take advantage of its provision to allow students to crossregister in other colleges and universities in the consortium.

Some faculty members from other disciplines were concerned that this would divert resources from their academic programs. I understood and assured them that this would not. Implementing these preprofessional programs would require minimal changes in the existing curricula. We would develop new marketing strategies to recruit students to Gallaudet. The first three preprofessional programs we implemented and incorporated into the curricula were medicine and health care, law, and business; the fourth one in architecture was still under development at the time of my retirement.

During my presidency, we established several new graduate programs, including a new doctoral program in interpretation and translation, to prepare both deaf and hearing students for careers as instructors and researchers in interpretation and translation. Likewise, we introduced a new doctoral program in educational neuroscience for students wanting to become research scientists in the field. Both programs were pioneers in their respective fields and, at that time, were one of a kind in the nation. We also created an innovative hybrid master's degree in sign language education, with two summer on-campus course sessions and a full academic year of online instruction for existing sign language teachers who aspired to advance in their field. We also developed a master's program in public administration in collaboration with the Federal Office of Personnel Management and American University to support deaf and hard of hearing individuals wanting to become leaders in governmental, private, and public agencies.

I felt fortunate to meet James Maguire, the founder and chair of the Philadelphia Insurance Companies, when he and I were graduation speakers at the Pennsylvania School for the Deaf in Philadelphia in 2013. He told the graduates a story about how he became a successful insurance agent when he became friends with a deaf family who lived in the same apartment building as he and his wife. He asked the deaf couple to introduce him to their deaf friends so that he could talk with them about getting the right kind of insurance for their families.

This small step led the Deaf community in Philadelphia to become a large part of his client base. Over time, he started his own insurance business, and it grew bigger and bigger. He told the graduates that he never forgot his roots; that is, the Deaf community played a big part in getting him started and becoming a successful leader in the insurance and risk management profession. Years later, he joined the board of directors at the Pennsylvania School for the Deaf and contributed over $2 million to build a new student life center.

After our graduation speeches, I asked him if he knew anything about Gallaudet University. He said, "No, please tell me about it." I was proud to talk about our great university and personally invited him and his wife, Frannie, to come for a visit. He was enthusiastic, so I immediately made plans for him, Frannie, and his management team to visit Gallaudet. I set up a meeting with the provost, deans, and faculty members in the Department of Business. We had a delightful discussion, and he told us about setting up the Maguire Insurance and Risk Management Institute at St. Joseph University in Philadelphia. He said he wanted to set up a similar program at Gallaudet because he believed that there would be tremendous prospects for young deaf people to pursue careers in insurance and risk management.

A delegation from Gallaudet traveled to Philadelphia to meet with the key leaders of the Maguire Risk Management and Insurance Institute at St. Joseph University. We received excellent information on how the program was set up at St. Joseph and took a tour of the campus facilities. Soon after, through Jim's leadership and generosity, Gallaudet University received a $500,000 grant from the Maguire Foundation to create a new Maguire Academy of Risk Management and Insurance. He also helped establish an advisory board of insurance and risk management leaders from the Washington, DC, metropolitan area to advise and guide Gallaudet in developing its program.

I came to know James well and to admire him. He was a strong-willed man with a clear vision. He's also a fitness-minded athlete who brought his entire family and many of his work colleagues into his fitness strategy. I appreciated that he was both goal- and action-oriented and a good listener who was incredibly generous.

The program he helped fund at Gallaudet enables interested students to receive training to fill many of the 400,000 jobs in the field of risk management and insurance that will open up as people retire in the next several years. As of this writing, several of the graduates from the Maguire Insurance and Risk Management Institute have been hired both as interns and permanent employees at the Philadelphia Insurance Companies. The university awarded him an honorary doctorate of business degree in May 2017.

SHORTLY AFTER ARRIVING at Gallaudet, I learned that the National Science Foundation (NSF) was questioning the status of Gallaudet's Visual Learning and Visual Language (VL2) as one of the NSF Science of Learning Centers. The NSF had awarded the university a major grant in 2005 to establish the VL2 program and had continued to support it financially in the years to follow. They were now worried that its goals were not being sufficiently met, even though faculty and students were conducting educational neuroscience research connected to deaf and hard of hearing students.

Since the VL2 program was at risk of losing its NSF funding, I worked closely with academic leaders to save the center. During several meetings with NSF officers, we asked for extra time to resurrect the program and seek a new leader for it.

This was not an easy process because the NSF officials were insistent on sticking to the original agreement with Gallaudet, which explicitly spelled out goals and established metrics to evaluate outcomes, but we managed to convince them. Based on Dr. Laura-Ann Petitto's many years of successful research leadership in the field of educational neuroscience and at the Brain and Language Lab (BL2) at the University of Toronto, we identified her as a prospective leader. She had also been the director of a similar center at Dartmouth College before her transfer to the University of Toronto. We shared this with the NSF, which said if we could bring Dr. Petitto to campus, they would reconsider and continue to fund VL2.

Dr. Carol Erting, then the dean of graduate and professional studies, and I worked very hard to negotiate with Dr. Petitto. When Dr. Petitto came on board, I emphasized the importance of her leadership in carrying out NSF's mandate to improve management of the Science of Learning Center and the VL2 project. I also impressed on her that a priority was to encourage multiple deaf and hard of hearing students at Gallaudet to become research scientists in educational neuroscience following in Dr. Petitto's footsteps.

To my delight, she met these objectives within five years. Today, several deaf students are doing well in the doctoral program in educational neuroscience. As of this writing, two of them completed their doctoral requirements in 2017 and 2018, respectively. NSF reported that it was extremely pleased with Dr. Petitto's leadership and performance and has continued to fund the project and even provided additional funding for other projects.

In 2012, it was time for Gallaudet to conduct once again its ten-year comprehensive review of its mission and academic programs for MSCHE reaccreditation. Academic leaders in consultation with the cabinet and myself formed a steering committee for a comprehensive self-study. The committee, per our agreement with MSCHE, chose a self-study group for its 2012–2013 review, which required that thirteen standards of the revised MSCHE *Characteristics of Excellence* be examined and reported. Gallaudet's five GSP goals served as the unifying and organizing framework for this self-study.

MSCHE commended the university for its candid approach to self-evaluation, and the openness with which the challenges of continuous improvement were shared. The community was also recognized for creating and sustaining a culture of assessment evident at all levels of the organization and governance structures.

I was proud of the work by the academic leaders, faculty and staff, and administration. I believe that the work done earlier by the two task forces helped to pave the way for a successful ten-year reaccreditation with the MSCHE commission.

Don Beil's stay at Gallaudet extended to one year, then the second, and onward to the third. One day toward the end of his fourth year as my chief of staff, he said, "Every time I go to California, it gets harder and harder for me to come back to Washington."

I understood, I said. "I'm so grateful you stayed with me longer than expected. Go be with your family."

He had played a significant role in our many achievements. Instead of hiring a replacement, I divided and assigned Don's responsibilities to five different individuals for the remaining two years of my term.

"THE DORMS ARE SHABBY," and "Would it be possible for our dorms to be nicer?" and "It's my least favorite thing about Gallaudet," were some of the comments I heard about campus life during my interviews with the Gallaudet community in September 2009. It seemed to be a consensus: Student housing was due for an upgrade and expansion. Dean for Student Life Dwight Benedict and his team were among those letting me know that Gallaudet needed new dorms. In a meeting with senior academic officers, one challenged me directly: "What are you going to do about the dorm situation?"

"Well," I said, "I do have some experience with private fundraising, and we had some success with that." Such fundraising had paid for the construction of the CSD Student Development Center at NTID. I'd had the good fortune to see firsthand how RIT's senior vice president for finance and administration managed to secure funds through governmental bond issues, which allowed us to move forward with a comprehensive campus improvement plan and the construction of over 220 new buildings and structures.

"That will never happen here, though," the Gallaudet dean said. "That idea has been discussed here for years, and still nothing has come of it."

During the interview process for the Gallaudet presidency, I had asked if Gallaudet had ever pursued a bond issue for campus improvement. When I learned that this had never been done, I shared RIT's success in this area and added that if I were to become president, I would put the vice president in touch with the RIT vice president and help facilitate communication.

Upon my election as president, I brought the bond issue concept up immediately with Paul Kelly, vice president for administration and finance, who was receptive. I then asked Don Beil to work with Paul to continue the discussion, and we pulled in some key members of the board's finance committee to explore this concept. Fortunately, several had considerable experience with bond issues and were enthusiastic. Other members of the finance committee helpfully provided their insights and critique.

We knew the days of getting construction funds from the federal government was a thing of the past, so obtaining a bond issue became an excellent alternative source of funding. The finance committee members decided to come up with a $40 million request. This would allow the university to build a new dormitory for $18 million. Then some of the remaining funds would be used to upgrade the other five dorms and renovate three Faculty Row houses. The remainder of the proposed funding would implement energy conservation strategies, including a new geothermal field. Improving the Field House facilities for athletes and installing new turf fields were also included in the plan. The proposal was then presented to and approved by the board of trustees. The bond development was a long, tedious, yet exciting process that required a full review and authorization by various banking and investment sources for bond issues. Gallaudet received strong ratings in the multi-As by two significant bond rating agencies.

Once approved, Gallaudet posted a notice through the financial agencies for a bond issue in anticipation that it would take several weeks or months to achieve our goal of $40 million. To our amazement, it took only twenty minutes to reach $20 million; by the end of the day, we had achieved the final goal of $40 million. It was indeed a new era for the university. In hindsight, we could have aimed for more money, but it was a good starting point.

As required by the DC zoning commission, Gallaudet developed a ten-year 2022 campus master plan. The plan included the construction projects outlined in the bond issue. The university implemented a creative budgeting process through annual depreciations that allowed us to improve the dormitory facilities. The new dormitory, Living and Learning Residence Hall #6, was completed within eighteen months, and students moved in by the fall of 2012. Renovation of the five existing dormitories, Faculty Row houses, academic labs and offices, and athletic facilities took place over the next few years.

An in-house architect, Mr. Hansel Bauman, executed a master campus plan and oversaw the design and building of all the construction projects according to a framework that allowed students, faculty, and staff to become engaged in the campus planning process with their insights and input. Each of these construction projects and renovations incorporated DeafSpace design elements. DeafSpace is an architectural design concept of utilizing open space in a way that touches on significant points within the deaf experience. It is all about resolving the five main challenge areas for deaf people: space, proximity, light, color, and acoustics.

As a part of the master plan, the university installed a new gate with a crosswalk leading to the new Union Market across the street from the campus. The plan's motto, "Transformation from Isolation to Innovation," looked to create opportunities for students, staff, and faculty through employment, internships, training, and collaborations in the surrounding community. During my tenure, I saw our students open up to the neighboring community and vice versa. We installed a Capital Bikeshare station, which allowed the Gallaudet community and those in the nearby community to pick up and drop off rental bikes that could be ridden to and from hundreds of other Bikeshare stations around the DC metropolitan area.

Overall, the campus transformation was dramatic. Over just a few years, Gallaudet went from a place where students regularly complained about their dorms to one where the dorms were beautiful, energy-efficient, safer, more accessible, and built to last for a very long time—set on a campus that had become more convenient and more welcoming.

19

Difficult Decisions

IN MY SECOND MONTH at Gallaudet, Dr. Ann Powell, a biology professor who had chaired President Davila's diversity team, made an appointment to speak with me. In her role as diversity team chair under my predecessor, she'd led a group of faculty, students, and administrative leaders who administered a diversity website, held open meetings on topics related to race and ethnicity and sexual orientation and gender, and advised the Office of the President on diversity initiatives.

"We should have a senior administrator in charge of diversity and inclusion," she told me. Fairness, openness, accommodation, celebrating differences, and overcoming bias and discrimination—these were all crucial issues facing every American university, Gallaudet included. She felt that we should follow the national trend of having a senior leader dedicated to guiding the institution's work in those areas. I agreed, and after discussing how that position might work and who the person occupying it should report to, the provost and I decided that a chief diversity officer (CDO) would serve in a dual role. They would be both associate provost for diversity in academic affairs, reporting to the provost, and assistant to the president for diversity and inclusion, reporting to me. It was an arrangement that we felt would reflect how vital diversity and inclusion was to so many aspects of the university's health—social, cultural, financial, public relations, and academic.

To fill such a significant, highly public role, we set up a committee to conduct a national search, hoping and expecting that leaders with both ASL proficiency and extensive experience in diversity leadership and management from around the country would apply.

One of the finalists was a beloved member of Gallaudet's own staff, Angela McCaskill, who had the distinction of being the first Black woman to earn a PhD at Gallaudet. She had been on the staff at Gallaudet for more than twenty years in various roles, from student services to academic advising.

A Howard graduate, her Gallaudet doctorate was in special education administration. She'd worked for the US Department of Education to oversee the states' implementation of IDEA and as a research associate for the VL2 project that was funded by the NSF. Overall, Dr. McCaskill was academically impressive but had limited experience in coordinating diversity programs. The provost and I believed, though, that she would be an outstanding leader of diversity for Gallaudet. What she lacked in directly related experience she could learn on the job, with our support.

Over a short period, Dr. McCaskill made excellent progress and established several workshops, panels, and open forums related to diversity on campus. She brought in consultants to help the university to achieve its diversity goals, which included enrolling more minority students, achieving a higher retention and graduation rate among minority students, and making our faculty more diverse. She also established a large advisory board of community leaders from the campus and outside campus as well. With feedback from the advisory board and her consultants, she developed a strategic plan that was enthusiastically supported by the university. Because her staff was small, I provided some of my staff from the Office of the President to support the program. Everything was going well and moving in the right direction. I was pleased and looked forward to her continuing progress.

In October 2012, just over a year into her assignment, two faculty members came to my office to report something they found alarming. They had just discovered that Dr. McCaskill's name was listed on a public petition to demand a vote—a referendum—to uphold or strike down the Civil Marriage Protection Act, which legalized same-sex marriage in Maryland and had been signed into law in March 2012.

"She should issue a public apology," they argued, "to the university." I indicated to them that I fully understood their concern about a high-level member of the administration taking what could be considered an antitolerance and antidiversity stand in such a public way.

"I'll speak with her," I said. "And would you be willing to meet with her to discuss your concern after I have had the opportunity to discuss the issue with her?"

Yes, they said they'd be willing, but they also insisted that a public apology to the community be issued first before they'd attend any meetings.

After they left my office, I sat for a while alone at my desk, filled with anxiety and disappointment. I agreed with the two professors. Dr. McCaskill's signature on that petition seemed like a rash and inflammatory act. While a diversity officer has the right to vote however she wants, live her private life how she wants, and even express her personal political opinions in private, I felt that the public nature of her role as the university's face on issues relating to diversity and equity meant that she should not make any public statements—which is what signing a public petition amounted to—that would conflict with the university's own diversity and inclusion stances and ideals.

I emailed her and asked her to meet with me to discuss what I'd learned. She wanted to meet with the two professors to defend herself, and discuss with them her ideas of how to address the issue of the petition with the Gallaudet community.

I encouraged Dr. McCaskill and the two professors to meet without my presence so that they could talk freely without my interference. I was hoping they would air their thoughts and feelings, make concessions, and admit that the other side had valid points. And I wanted them to draw a road map out of the mess, something that we could all agree to.

To my dismay, they could not resolve the conflict. Neither side was willing to make amends or come up with a compromise that would meet both of their satisfactions. Soon, rumors spread throughout campus, making a resolution both more difficult and more urgently needed. I decided to temporarily suspend Dr. McCaskill, with pay, from her position in the administration, so that I could ask the appropriate individuals to investigate the situation and advise me. By now, news of the petition and her signature was known everywhere. Many LGBTQ students were angry and concerned. In my office, we had a series of dialogues with students, faculty, and staff about how the incident might either positively or negatively affect the student body.

Students sat around the table in my office and sobbed. Others angrily described their feelings that the university itself was abandoning their rights. "If you say you're willing to put my rights to spend my life with the person I love up for a popular vote, then you don't really believe I have rights!"

With her lawyer, Dr. McCaskill held a televised news conference two days later. She described her feelings about receiving my email informing her of my decision to place her on leave: "I was shocked, hurt, insulted. I was humiliated," she said. I watched her on the television screen from my living room, with Vicki, and my heart sank. Dr. McCaskill argued that she wasn't "anti-gay" but rather "pro-democracy." She listed the actions she'd taken as Gallaudet's CDO to further the cause of LGBTQ equality—opening an LGBTQ student center, hiring an openly transgender person to her staff, and holding forums and other events with LGBTQ themes. She characterized my suspending her as "intimidation," and the complaints and threats from the two faculty members who had complained about her as "bullying."

It was an emotional and trying time for me. The LGBTQ students and faculty felt attacked by the referendum to put their rights up for a vote, and they felt disrespected by the very person whose job it was to advocate for them. On the other hand, many other students and faculty of color and many religious students felt that my disciplining of Dr. McCaskill was rash and overly harsh. Even some gay and lesbian leaders among the students and faculty criticized me for suspending her, arguing that doing so violated her right to free speech and was an overreach.

The irony stung. I could see the merits of the freedom-of-speech arguments against me. After all, I had very recently asserted that same argument in my defense of the *Corpus Christi* play, offensive to some Christian students.

Then-governor of Maryland, Martin O'Malley, a strong proponent of marriage equality rights, made a statement criticizing my suspension of Dr. McCaskill and calling for her reinstatement. It seemed that I was caught in the middle of a storm, and everything I did to batten something down in the wind allowed for something else to be whipped away. I was making no one happy, it seemed. My old mentor's advice to me—that I should worry less about what anyone thought of me—felt useless in those weeks. Whether I worried about perceptions of me or not didn't seem to matter. Amid such hurt feelings, conflicting opinions, and conflicting principles, any decision I made would be met with an outcry.

In bed that night, I tried to shut off all thoughts of Gallaudet. I wanted just a few hours of peace. I wanted the heavy dread that seemed to press lately on my chest to lift. Our cat, Sophia, jumped up onto our bed and stalked across my legs and Vicki's, up my torso, and nestled between our heads. I reached over to pet her striped cheeks, and she returned my gaze serenely, as cats do. *She* didn't have a care in the world. "I should try to be more like Sophia tomorrow," I joked to Vicki. She laughed and agreed, but pointed out that Sophia didn't have any direct reports, let alone a large university to lead.

After several months of meetings with key leaders at the university and the board, I ultimately made the decision to remove Dr. Mc-Caskill from her position and relocate her to an academic department as a faculty member that would be commensurate with her experience and training.

From the beginning to the end of this issue, I kept the board of trustees informed and met with the board chair to apprise him of the situation in our weekly videoconference calls. I believed it was resolved in the best interest of the university and the students, although it was one of the most unpleasant and disillusioning experiences in my career as an administrator.

Afterward, I worked with a consultant to develop a new position description for the next CDO with considerable and comprehensive involvement of various constituencies on campus, including faculty, staff, and students in open community-wide forums. A new position description was drafted and shared with the community, including governance leaders (e.g., the faculty council, staff council, student body government, graduate students association, and board of trustees). Prior to my retirement in December 2015, the position description was posted with the expectation that the next president of Gallaudet would select the new CDO.

20

Heart Troubles

As USUAL, I was short of breath. It was my asthma, I thought. I'd been dealing with asthma for the past fifteen years, but now the medicines didn't seem to work anymore. I insisted on taking a stress test, even though I had taken stress tests a few times before, and they had been inconclusive.

"You look like you're having difficulty breathing," the nurse watching me said. "I'm going to ask you to get off the treadmill right now." The doctor ordered a CAT scan, which was inconclusive.

My cardiologist, Dr. Morris, suggested an angiogram test with the plans to put in a stent or two the next day.

"But we have plans," I said. "I'm the graduation speaker at a school for the deaf in Arizona this weekend. We fly out in a few days."

Dr. Morris shook his head. "I'm afraid delaying the angiogram would be a risk, Dr. Hurwitz."

The angiogram procedure the next day, a Friday, revealed that I had four blocked arteries, two eighty-percent blockages, and two ninety-percent blockages. I needed to have bypass surgery right away. Dr. Wagman met with Vicki in the waiting room and explained the results to her, noting that I would be in the intensive care unit afterward. Vicki held back her tears because there were other people in the room. After a few minutes, she was told she could see me. Dr. Wagman said the surgery would take place the following Monday morning.

"Good," I told him, "I'll spend the weekend at home and come back Monday."

He said, "No, no—you are staying here for the weekend so that you can be prepared for the surgery Monday morning." Although I was taken aback, Vicki was relieved. "What were you thinking?" she admonished me when we were alone.

We contacted our children. Bernard flew down to be with us on the day of my surgery, and though Stephanie wanted to join us, we insisted she stay at work so that she wouldn't lose her pay.

I had to cancel five major trips, including one to Brazil and Argentina that summer, since the cardiologist commanded that I not travel until the fall. And the annual "Bike with the President" tour, which we'd enjoyed doing with students and alumni, faculty, and staff, biking from campus to Alexandria and then Georgetown and Capitol Hill, had to be canceled too.

As they brought the gurney to my room to wheel me to surgery, I said, "I'll walk," an idea that was completely ignored by everyone in the room.

After the surgery, I was moved to the recovery room. Vicki and Bernard were brought in while I was asleep. My first words upon waking were, "Please give me my pager." Vicki initially refused, but after my insistence, she gave up. A few minutes later, my surgeon came into the recovery room and said, "How are you feeling?" Although I don't remember saying this, Vicki and Bernard were amused by my answer: "I'm ready for work!"

An NTID colleague sent me a message expressing his thoughts about my recovery, and I responded right away. He was shocked and told everyone in his hallway about getting my instant response just a few hours after my open-heart surgery.

When a nurse entered to check my vitals and the IV drip, I am reported to have said to her: "Please replace the sign 'hearing impaired' with 'D-E-A-F.' 'Hearing impaired' makes it sound like my ears are broken. My ears aren't broken. I just don't hear."

Vicki leaned in, her beautiful face etched with worry. "Are you in pain?" she asked me. "What do you expect!" I retorted.

When Dr. Boyce came in to check on me after the surgery, he said rather nonchalantly, "You know, you never had asthma all those years. It was all your heart."

"Are you joking?" Vicki and I both asked at once, taken aback.

He said, "No, not at all. Your heart is fine now, and you don't need to take albuterol any longer!"

At home in House One, Vicki took excellent care of me. That required patience! I was always complaining about one thing after another. Once I was able to walk up the stairs (eighty steps from the first floor to the third floor), the nurse who visited daily stopped coming.

When I went to see Dr. Boyce for a checkup after six weeks, he told me I could do anything I wanted to, including drive. I complained of chest discomfort, which he explained was the result of my ribs that had to be sawed down the middle and pulled outward so that he could work on my heart. That did explain the soreness.

I was able to maintain my work responsibilities while recuperating at home. Some of my direct reports came to House One to meet with me about critical issues and to keep me updated on campus issues and challenges. I also kept up with emails daily. Over time, my cardiologist encouraged me to gradually increase my time in the office. Within a few weeks, I was back to my normal self, although I continued to go to rehabilitation. But would I ever be able to fulfill my bucket list ambition to bike the five boroughs of New York City in one day? In May 2015, I achieved that dream when I cycled forty-two miles through the boroughs, over the Brooklyn Bridge, with the Statue of Liberty who had welcomed some of my grandparents over my shoulder, through leafy Queens, and around the southern tip of Manhattan.

21

Farewell to Gallaudet

As I prepared to step down at the end of my six-year presidency on December 31, 2015, I embraced what I refer to as the culmination of my fifty-plus years of professional work. I was both honored and humbled that Vicki and I were featured in the fall 2015 issue of *Gallaudet Today*. The article, "President Hurwitz's Legacy: Bridging the Past toward the Future," talked about how I had facilitated a transformation in academics, research, technology, and campus enhancements. It also included a heartwarming description of Vicki's passion for volunteer service during her tenure.

In honor of my retirement, the board of trustees hosted the STEM Matters Symposium. Dr. Jorge Diaz Herrera, Gallaudet board member and president of Keuka College, was the keynote speaker and spoke about the future of STEM (science, technology, engineering, and mathematics) and evolving technologies in higher education, business, and industry. Other speakers included Phil Bravin, Jim DeCaro—past interim president and dean emeritus of NTID—and Provost Carol Erting. Professors Regina Nuzzo, Caroline Solomon, and Paul Sabilia each gave a demonstration of how mathematics, biology, and chemistry could be taught to students at Gallaudet. I was the endnote speaker. I discussed the value of STEM education for students at Gallaudet University.

Three presidents at my retirement party: Robert Davila, Roberta "Bobbi" Cordano, and myself.

Following the symposium, dozens of brilliant students showcased their STEM research to the campus in a poster show and demonstration. As I surveyed their impressive displays and stopped to speak with the young people, my heart filled with love, pride, and hope for their future careers. Gone are the days when deaf children are left in the apartment above the family store, as my father and his sister had been, unchallenged and uneducated. Although it may appear that the days when the hearing world discounts the full humanity and contributions of the Deaf community are gone, we still have a long way to make our society fully accessible to Deaf, hard of hearing, and Deaf-Blind people and people with disabilities.

My trusted colleague, Don Beil, my wonderful chief of staff the first four years of my presidency, said in an interview: "President Hurwitz met with hundreds of students during his totally student-centered leadership of Gallaudet University. This, alone, and without intention, provided them contact with an outstanding role model who proves repeatedly the value of a full education, the value of hard work, and the value of developing leadership and managerial skills. His has also been a life of service. . . . Educated as an engineer, he entered the field of education of deaf people, creating a successful career in preparing students for their futures in a complex, compound world demanding a wide composite set of skills for success. I believe his continued extensive work with students across the campus has encouraged students to learn and make service a part of their lives."

Vicki and I cherished our time with students both on- and off-campus when we traveled to Gallaudet-sponsored regional academic bowls for high school students. We hosted many student events at House One. We loved attending many student athletic games. We also enjoyed going to their performances at Eastman Theatre and dance shows at Foster Auditorium. We will never forget the trip we took with a group of eighty students during their eight-day First Year Experience educational trip to Costa Rica in 2012, and how we enjoyed zip lining with them.

DEAF PEOPLE OF COLOR, a group of faculty and staff members of color, asked Vicki and I to be involved with a fundraising event, "Dancing with the Gallaudet Stars." Vicki was thrilled because she loved dancing, but I freaked out. I never could learn how to dance and often claimed that I had two left feet. Vicki persuaded me to be a good sport and try my best. She had always wanted me to take dancing lessons with her but I had always managed to avoid it. She reminded me that we both did some crazy rum-fueled dancing during my fraternity years at Washington University.

I panicked even more when we learned that each of us would have a different partner. Vicki paired up with Fred Beam, an extremely talented choreographer and dancer. My partner was Nathalie Pluviose, an amazing young deaf woman, who was a professional dancer and a remarkable dance teacher.

Nathalie patiently taught me some basic dance steps. As we repeated them, I kept forgetting the previous steps and would mess up. She kept smiling, and encouraged me to keep learning. I was a bit intimidated when she said we had to do sixty different steps for our performance. I kept making mistakes, but we somehow made it to sixty steps. She surprised me by saying that we needed to learn a second

*Zip lining with Gallaudet students in Costa
Rica.*

dance with sixty additional steps! Flustered, I kept mixing up steps
between both routines. It took me weeks before I could successfully
get through each dance.

The evening of the performance finally arrived, and as I was back-
stage trying to remember all 120 different steps, I kept mixing them
up. Nathalie and I were called to the stage for an interview with the
judges. Each of the star dancers had previously made a video with a
brief explanation of our dancing experience, which was shown to the
audience before we began our dancing performances. In my video, I
mentioned that it was a learning experience for me while struggling
with my two left feet.

Nathalie and I performed our two routines. I was astounded that
I was able to perform with ease—something I credit entirely to Nathalie. She was wonderful and gave me a lot of cues to move on to the

subsequent steps. When we completed our performances, we stood next to the judges for their comments. One of them, WaWa Snipes, stood up and exclaimed that I had been lying the whole time about my lack of dancing skills.

Vicki and her partner, Fred Beam, placed third in the contest. Although Nathalie and I didn't place, the experience gave me the confidence to perform on a stage other than simply to give a lecture or a speech. Vicki was thrilled to see that I did have some rhythm after all.

ONE OF THE HIGHLIGHTS during my tenure at Gallaudet University was when Vicki and I were invited by President Barack and First Lady Michelle Obama to be their guests at the annual Chanukah reception at the White House. This was largely due to Leah Katz-Hernandez, a Gallaudet alumna, who served as the White House receptionist, putting us on the invitation list. There were over five hundred people, many of who were representatives, senators, and significant leaders

President and First Lady Obama and President and First Lady Hurwitz at the White House Chanukah reception.

from all over the United States. US Supreme Court Justice Ruth Bader Ginsburg, Vice President Joe Biden and his wife, Dr. Jill Biden, were among the guests we saw. The food was great with a lot of Jewish delicacies, including mini-lamb chops, latkes, and wine imported from Israel. After the president spoke to the audience, we were instructed to go to the lower level for a photo shoot with both President Obama and First Lady Obama. After waiting in a long line, we finally came up to the Obamas with our interpreter. When I introduced myself to President Obama, he said that Gallaudet had been doing a remarkable job. I reminded him that each year he and I cosigned diplomas for all graduating students as is normally done by US presidents (Howard University is the only other university that has this honor). I then commented to First Lady Michelle that I understood that she was a notetaker for a deaf student at Whitney Young High School in Chicago. She brightened and said in sign, "I know sign language and my name is Michelle!" She fingerspelled her name gracefully and without a hitch. The four of us posed in front of a fireplace for our photograph, an unforgettable experience.

NEAR THE CONCLUSION of my presidency in December 2015, I was approached by a rabbi who advised us to have the mezuzahs removed from House One should the selected president not be Jewish. Vicki and I were not sure what to do about the mezuzahs but considered donating them to the Gallaudet archives. Later, President-Designate Roberta "Bobbi" Cordano and her wife, Mary Baremore, persuaded us not to remove the mezuzahs because they wanted House One to continue being blessed. Vicki and I were both pleased and gratified.

I often tell people that serving as a university president was like being a small-town mayor with multiple responsibilities. I was ultimately responsible for everything that happened on campus. That entailed leading an academic institution for a comprehensive K–12 school, university academic and student affairs, student/faculty/staff governance groups, student housing, facilities, food services, library services, a hotel, landscaping, snow removals, construction, and parking lots. The board of trustees, to whom I reported to, was like a city council, a governing body. It was a fantastic experience, and I enjoyed working with everyone in different capacities at all levels.

I want to be remembered for my resiliency, integrity, tireless work ethic, business acumen, and respect for openness, flexibility, and diversity. I'd also like to be recognized for my student centeredness, my authentic commitment to Gallaudet University's bilingual mission, and my steady, consistent emphasis on quality education and service, research, and outreach. Has it been a walk through the park? No, it hasn't. There were challenges at every step along the way, but everyone at the university worked together to make tremendous progress.

During the last summer at Gallaudet, when Vicki and I traveled to Greece and Turkey for the International Congress for Education of the Deaf and World Federation of the Deaf conferences, we spent two weeks in Italy in celebration of our fiftieth wedding anniversary between the conferences. We rented a car and drove to Rome, along a winding highway to sunny Naples, out to the rolling countryside near Siena and through Siena's ancient stone streets, to art-filled Florence, and from magical Venice to the businesslike Milan. And in April 2017, we traveled to Berlin/Potsdam, Germany, to celebrate the seventieth birthday of our friends, Asger and Ritva Bergmann, from Copenhagen, Denmark, with forty friends from different countries.

"We are blessed," I said to Vicki as we strolled home to our hotel, after the lively dinner in Potsdam. As I often do, I thought of my parents, with all of their intelligence and optimism and hard work. Wouldn't they be happy to see how far education and opportunities had brought their son? Vicki often tells me, "Your parents would be as proud of you today as they always were!"

I continue to have high hopes for Gallaudet's future. It is important for the university to keep up with the changing world and be on the cutting edge. There will be challenges, but there are good people on campus equal to those challenges. Gallaudet has an excellent board of trustees and a vibrant community. I strongly believe Gallaudet has a bright future ahead and many more lives to lift and shape. And even more important, the lives of deaf people all across America and around the world continue to improve as technology and education improve, as possibilities expand, and as more and more of us have a chance to reach our full potential.